MW01076104

CHRIST TRIUMPHS OVER
SIN AND DEATH

A GIFT FROM

GRACE
to You

GTY.ORG

Christ Triumphs over Sin and Death: The King's Victorious Return
Copyright © 2025 by John MacArthur. All rights reserved. No portion of this
book may be reproduced in any form without the written permission of the
copyright owner, except for brief excerpts quoted in critical reviews.

Content in this book has been adapted from the forthcoming
commentary *Daniel*, The MacArthur Old Testament Commentary
(Los Angeles: The Master's Seminary Press, 2025).
Copyright © 2025 by John MacArthur.
Used by permission. All rights reserved.

Scripture quotations are taken from the (LSB®) Legacy Standard Bible®,
Copyright © 2021 by The Lockman Foundation.
Managed in partnership with Three Sixteen Publishing Inc. LSBible.org.
Used by permission. All rights reserved.

DESIGNED BY WEKREATIVE CO.
ISBN: 978-1-883973-11-7
PRINTED IN CHINA

CHRIST TRIUMPHS OVER SIN AND DEATH

THE KING'S VICTORIOUS RETURN

JOHN MACARTHUR

CONTENTS

INTRODUCTION

All Scripture is God-breathed and spiritually profitable for the salvation and sanctification of every believer. Every word of God is pure truth, living and life-giving, powerful and empowering.

For over half a century, I have lived daily with the Scripture in my hands and on my mind, preaching through all of the New Testament and many portions of the Old Testament from the pulpit of the church. This work in the Word has resulted in a full series of expository commentaries on each New Testament book, totaling thirty-four volumes, and a number of commentaries on various books of the Old Testament.

I am grateful for everyone who is willing to settle in and dig deep in reading a commentary. But only a few take on such an extensive journey, even though every aspect of the Scripture is life transforming. My desire, however, is for many to engage in such a pursuit because they will then experience the benefit and blessing of the deep dive into a biblical book.

I am certain when people have a taste of the riches of Bible exposition they will want more. So I thought we should give them less to develop the hunger for more.

What do I mean by less?

ONE CHAPTER. ONE MONUMENTAL CHAPTER.

So, that led to the development of this series, *The Great Chapters of the Bible*. This series focuses on key portions of Scripture that establish the foundational truths of the Christian faith. The current volume, focusing on Daniel 9, from the forthcoming commentary on Daniel in The MacArthur Old Testament Commentary series, depicts the glorious sovereignty of God over the history of Israel and the triumph of Christ over sin and death.

I believe that exposition of the great chapters of the Bible will lead many to desire to know the rest of each book and to experience the blessing of knowing the Scripture in its fullness.

01

A MAN OF PRAYER

DANIEL 9:1–3

n the first year of Darius the son of Ahasuerus, from the seed of the Medes, who was made king over the kingdom of the Chaldeans—in the first year of his reign, I, Daniel, discerned in the books the number of the years *concerning* which the word of Yahweh came to Jeremiah the prophet for the fulfillment of the laying waste of Jerusalem, *namely*, seventy years. So I gave my face to the Lord God to seek *Him* by prayer and supplications, with fasting, sackcloth, and ashes.

Scripture resounds with compelling examples of persistent and powerful prayer. Abraham interceded for the righteous remnant living in Sodom, ultimately trusting that the Judge of all the earth would do what is right (Gen 18:23–32). Jacob wrestled all night with the Angel of the LORD, refusing to let go until he received a blessing from God (32:22–32; Hos 12:3). Moses interceded on behalf of the disobedient Israelites, pleading with the Lord to show mercy for the sake of His great name (Exod 33:12–23). Hannah cried out to the Lord on account of her infertility, promising to dedicate her child into His service (1 Sam 2:1–10). Agonizing over his sin with Bathsheba, David petitioned the Lord for spiritual cleansing and restoration (Ps 51). Solomon asked the Lord for wisdom, which God was pleased to give him (2 Chr 1:11–12). Moments after asking God to send down fire from heaven, Elijah prayed for rain to end Israel's drought (1 Kgs 18:41–19:8). The rebellious prophet Jonah, from the belly of a fish, begged for mercy (Jonah 2). The Lord Jesus petitioned His Father with tears to do His will on the night before His death (Matt 26:36–46). After being threatened by the religious leaders, Peter and the other apostles prayed for courage and strength (Acts 4:29–30). The Apostle Paul instructed believers to pray without ceasing (1 Thess 5:17). In every case, the power behind effective praying was not the words uttered, but the God to whom they were directed. God delights in answering the prayers of His people when according to His will (Prov 15:29), as He causes all things to work together for His glory and the good of those who belong to Him (Rom 8:28).

One of the most exemplary prayers in the Bible is recorded in Daniel 9. Throughout his life, the prophet exhibited spiritual excellence in many categories—including profound wisdom (Dan 1:20), enduring courage (e.g., 1:8–21; 6), impeccable trustworthiness (e.g., 2:48; 5:29; 6:3), and unwavering faithfulness to the Lord (6:5). In addition to these notable qualities, chapter 9 reveals Daniel to be a man of earnest prayer. His example warrants careful consideration, since prayer must be a vital part of every believer's life (cf. Eph 6:18). The believer is to pray for others (Jas 5:16), to pray in faith (1:6), and to pray fervently

(5:17). He is to pray for fruitful ministry (2 Thess 3:1) and always for the glory of God (Ps 115:1; John 14:13).

Throughout his life, Daniel exemplified steadfast commitment to prayer. In chapter 6, he refused to stop praying even at the risk of being thrown into a den of lions. Rather than cower in fear, he continued in faith, kneeling openly before God and worshiping Him (Dan 6:10). Daniel offered the prayer recorded in this chapter (Dan 9) in the same year as the events of Daniel 6—the first year of Darius (6:1; 9:1). While Daniel 6 revealed the courage Daniel displayed in his praying, Daniel 9 features the monumental content of one of his prayers. In this prayer, Daniel displayed wholehearted dependence on the sovereignty of God as well as a deep sense of the sinfulness that marked him and his people. As one of the richest Old Testament passages on prayer, Daniel 9:1–19 provides a model for subsequent generations of believers to emulate.

The first three verses of this chapter set the stage for Daniel's prayer and the Lord's answer. Daniel recognized the sovereign providence of God (v. 1) and rested in the prophetic promises of Scripture (v. 2). With his confidence anchored in the Lord and His Word, Daniel responded in penitent supplication— seeking God's face in humble prayer (v. 3). Daniel's life modeled the devotion and dependence that should characterize the prayers of every believer. Accordingly, the Lord was pleased to answer (vv. 22–27), revealing to Daniel the glories of Israel's future. While Daniel offered this prayer out of specific concern in Israel's history, God's answer foretold events extending all the way into the eschatological kingdom of Christ.

RECOGNIZING GOD'S SOVEREIGN PROVIDENCE

In the first year of Darius the son of Ahasuerus, from the seed of the Medes, who was made king over the kingdom of the Chaldeans ... (9:1)

At the age of eighty, and after a lifetime in exile, Daniel longed for God to return the people of Israel from Babylon to Judah. At the end of the previous chapter, Daniel expressed his anguish on account of God's revelation about Israel's future suffering (Dan 8:27). Twelve years had elapsed since then. Yet, Daniel continued to seek further understanding about what awaited his people, appealing to the Lord in prayer and confident that God's sovereign purposes would be accomplished (cf. Ps 115:3; Dan 4:25; 7:9).

Daniel introduced this prayer by setting the historical context, explaining that these events took place **in the first year of Darius the son of Ahasuerus,** that is in 539 BC. **Darius** is most likely an honorific title for King Cyrus (cf. Dan 5:31; 6:28), ruler of Medo-Persia and conqueror of Babylon (cf. Dan 5:31). He was the **son of Ahasuerus,** also a royal title. Though Cyrus was Persian by ethnicity, he assumed a Median title and was even considered to be **from the seed of the Medes,** meaning they counted him as their own. Deeply respected by both the Medes and the Persians, Darius successfully united these two nations to form the Medo-Persian empire. This conglomerate appeared several times throughout Daniel's prophecies, being depicted by the two silver arms of the image in Daniel 2, the lopsided bear in Daniel 7, and the ram with two horns in Daniel 8. The ram's horns represented Media and Persia respectively, symbolizing their unification into a single empire (cf. 8:20). These prophecies and their fulfilment served as a reminder to Daniel, and by extension to every believer, that God is sovereign over all of history and that He orchestrates every event according to His perfect purposes.

Daniel also noted that Darius **was made king over the kingdom of the Chaldeans.** That Darius *was* **made king** reflected the reality that his reign was appointed and established by God, just as the prophets had foretold (cf. Dan 2:39; Isa 44:28; 45:1). Because he recognized God's sovereign hand at work (cf. Dan 9:12), Daniel's prayers were marked by confidence and fervency. Daniel sought the Lord in prayer knowing that both international powers and his personal circumstances were in God's mighty hand.

In recognizing that Darius became king **over the kingdom of the Chaldeans,** Daniel would have been reminded of God's protection over him. Daniel had a long tenure as a senior member in the government of the Babylonians (Dan 5:11; 10:1). The night that Medo-Persia overthrew Babylon, he was not killed. Instead, he was made third in command (5:29). Daniel not only survived the regime change but also retained his prominence in the new government. While this speaks to his exceptional character, it highlights an even greater truth—namely, that the Lord was faithful to care for Daniel during violent and tumultuous times. Daniel's confidence in prayer was buttressed by the fact that he had repeatedly witnessed God's providential care over his own life. Since the date of Daniel's prayer was **the first year of Darius the son of Ahasuerus,** this would have also been the year Daniel endured his epic trial in the lions' den (cf. 6:1). His actions demonstrated his commitment to prayer no matter the circumstances or potential dangers (cf. 6:10, 12). Absolutely convinced of God's sovereign love and covenant faithfulness, he withstood the pressure to compromise, resolving instead to seek the Lord in prayer.

RESTING IN SCRIPTURE'S PROMISES

... in the first year of his reign, I, Daniel, discerned in the books the number of the years *concerning* which the word of Yahweh came to Jeremiah the prophet for the fulfillment of the laying waste of Jerusalem, *namely*, seventy years. (9:2)

The motivation and content of Daniel's prayer was informed by his careful reading of God's Word. He explained that **in the first year of his reign, I, Daniel, discerned in the books the number of the years *concerning* which the word of Yahweh came to Jeremiah the prophet.** In repeating that it was **the first year of his** [Darius'] **reign,** Daniel connected the date not only with the historical circumstances but also with the fulfillment of prophecy. Nearly seventy years had passed since Daniel had been exiled. Daniel discovered the significance of that number by reading the book of Jeremiah (cf. Jer 25:11–12; 29:10).

He described himself as **I, Daniel,** an expression reflecting a sense of unworthiness that he would be given such revelatory insight from the Lord. As the prophet Isaiah revealed, the Lord is looking for those who tremble at His Word (cf. Isa 66:2), and Daniel repeatedly demonstrated that kind of God-honoring humility (cf. Dan 7:28; 8:15, 27).

Daniel's commitment to Scripture is reflected in the phrase **I … discerned in the books.** He did not merely read Scripture but he **discerned** the meaning of its message. He carefully considered, analyzed, and sought to understand its meaning. He committed himself to studying **the books,** the portions of the Old Testament that had been written up to that time. Though Daniel explicitly mentioned Jeremiah, understanding Jeremiah's prophecy required comprehending other Old Testament books as well. While Jeremiah revealed the duration of the exile, Daniel also needed to grasp when the exile began and why it occurred. To answer those questions, he needed to be familiar with Leviticus, Deuteronomy, 1–2 Kings, Psalms, and Isaiah—books Daniel even alluded to in his prayer (cf. Dan 9:7–19). Accordingly, Daniel's reading of Scripture must have been comprehensive and broad.

Daniel studied Scripture with meticulous precision, discerning **the** specific **number of the years concerning which the word of Yahweh came to Jeremiah the prophet.** Paying careful attention to the details, such as **the number of the years,** he understood that these details were **the word of Yahweh** which **came to Jeremiah the prophet.** Daniel understood that Scripture was divinely inspired (cf. Dan 2:20–23), accurate even to specific words and numbers. Jeremiah prophesied three times that

Israel's captivity in Babylon would last seventy years. Jeremiah 25:11 states that the land of Israel will be a wasteland and that the nation would serve Babylon for seventy years. Jeremiah 25:12 adds that after seventy years, God would punish Babylon, and in Jeremiah 29:10, the prophet foretold that when Babylon was destroyed, God would return His people to the Promised Land. So, as Daniel carefully read through the book of Jeremiah in the first year of Darius, he realized that the years denoted in the prophecy were nearly completed. Scripture became Daniel's counselor (Ps 119:24), informing his understanding of the times and prompting him to pray. As testified throughout Scripture, profound prayer results from a clear understanding of God's Word (cf. 19:7–14; 73:15–28; 119:2). Divine revelation compels the believer to seek the Lord in supplication (cf. Ezra 9:4–5; Eph 3:1–14).

Fervent prayer is also fueled by a desire to submit to God's will. In studying the Scripture, Daniel perceived God's timeline for **the fulfillment of the laying waste of Jerusalem,** *namely,* **seventy years.** For centuries, Israel had sinned by ignoring God's command to keep the sabbath (Exod 20:8; Deut 5:12), and to rest the land both on the sabbatical years (Lev 25:1–7) and on the years of Jubilee (25:8–22). Moses warned that if Israel failed to observe these commands, God would expel them out of the land and **lay waste** to their cities, including the capital city of **Jerusalem** (Lev 26:31, 33). In laying them waste, God ordained that these locations would lie dormant and uninhabited for several decades. Then the land would finally have its rest, making up for all the years that Israel failed to have sabbatical years and years of Jubilee to rest the land (26:34, 41, 43). In Israel's five hundred years as a kingdom, they missed about seventy sabbatical years, thus God decreed that they would spend **seventy years** in captivity in Babylon (cf. 2 Chr 36:21).

Daniel understood that the Israelites were under God's discipline as a result of their rebellion (Lev 26:14–43). Mourning for Jerusalem, habitually facing toward that city as he prayed for God's mercy (Dan 6:10; cf. 1 Kgs 8:35), Daniel also realized that the time of Israel's captivity was reaching its **fulfillment.** Just as Jeremiah had predicted, nearly seventy years had passed since Daniel was exiled in 605 BC, and Babylon had now been defeated. Recognizing that the circumstances necessary for Israel's return were coming together according to God's prophetic plan, Daniel responded by seeking the Lord in prayer.

Daniel illustrates that prayer should be according to God's will (cf. 1 John 5:14). Prayer does not change God's will, since He has planned the end from the beginning (cf. Isa 46:9–10). Rather, understanding God's will as revealed in Jeremiah's prophecy allowed Daniel to know how to pray as he interceded for his people (cf. 1 John 5:14–15). Because he rested in God's sovereign will, Daniel responded with praise for God's power and plan (cf. Isa 25:1; Eph 1:11). He prayed that his fellow Israelites would also be conformed to God's will (cf. Rom 12:2). Just as Elijah's prayer was effective because it was according to God's will (cf. 1 Kgs 17–18; Jas 5:16–18), for the same reason Daniel's prayer proved effective. The reality of God's sovereignty did not deter Daniel from praying. Rather, it fueled his confidence because he knew God would accomplish His purposes in every detail.

Daniel's example is consistent with other faithful believers who prayed according to the will of God. Samuel petitioned the Lord based on His will and promises (cf. 1 Sam 12:19–22). David similarly prayed, "I desire to do Your will, O my God" (Ps 40:8). The people of Ezra's day heartily affirmed God's will (Neh 8:6). Jesus taught that the disciples should pray, "Your kingdom come. Your will be done, on earth as it is in heaven" (Matt 6:10). Jesus Himself beseeched the Father, "Yet not My will, but Yours be done" (Luke 22:42). In the book of Revelation, John prayed "Amen. Come, Lord Jesus" (Rev 22:20). In the same way, Daniel prayed not to alter God's will but to participate in it. That is not to suggest that Daniel was a fatalist, claiming that divine sovereignty excused him of any responsibility. Instead, his recognition of God's will compelled him to conform to it fully and to pray accordingly. As illustrated by Daniel's example, effective prayer is grounded in God's Word and alignment with His will. Daniel knew that prayer is a means God uses to fulfill His will (Matt 6:9–10; 1 John 5:14).

RESPONDING WITH SUPPLICATION AND PENITENCE

So I gave my face to the Lord God to seek *Him by* prayer and supplications, with fasting, sackcloth, and ashes. (9:3)

Informed by divine revelation, Daniel **gave** his **face to the Lord God,** an expression denoting complete devotion (cf. Ezek 14:8; 15:7). In response to Israel's disobedience, God set His face against His people to chasten and exile them (cf. Lev 26:17). And in response to God's chastisement of Israel, Daniel set his face to seek the Lord in prayer. His unrelenting dedication to intercede stemmed from his burden for Israel and his confidence in both the revelation and lovingkindness of **the Lord God.** The term **Lord** (*Adonai*) is not the covenant name for God but the word that means *master*, emphasizing God's sovereignty. This divine title was used in the opening verses of the book (Dan 1:1–2) and appears ten times in chapter 9. Daniel's understanding of God's sovereign will both motivated and fortified his prayer. In appealing to Yahweh not only as **Lord** but also as **God,** the Sovereign who possesses all power, Daniel knew he was addressing the One who could never fail (cf. Job 42:2; Isa 55:10–11; Lam 3:21–24). Daniel's confidence in God's character fueled the fervency of his petition.

Daniel devoted himself **to seek *Him by* prayer and supplications.** While **prayer** can describe any act of speaking to the Lord in general, in this context the focus is on praise and confession. In Psalm 86:5–6, David pleaded that God would hear his prayer because He is a forgiving God. In Psalm 143:1–2, David also petitioned the Lord to hear his prayer and not to enter into judgment against him. In like manner, Daniel offered a prayer of repentance. He entered God's presence with sincere contrition (cf. Ps 51:3–5; Matt 6:12; Luke 18:13). In addition to confession, Daniel also sought the Lord with **supplications,** a term derived from the Hebrew root for grace. Turning to the Lord, Daniel depended on His grace and desperately pleaded for God to intervene for him and for the nation. Many years prior to Daniel, Solomon had prayed that the Lord would do justice for His people in exile when they offered "their prayer and their supplication" toward the temple (1 Kgs 8:45). The Lord affirmed that this was His very will (9:3). So with **prayer and supplications,** Daniel acted in precise accordance with what God had prescribed.

Daniel evidenced his earnestness by accompanying his prayer **with fasting, sackcloth, and ashes.** He understood that **fasting** is neither meritorious nor an end in itself (cf. Isa 58:3–7; Zech 7; Matt 6:16–18). Rather, fasting reveals an intense focus, often stemming from an urgent situation that eliminates any desire for food (cf. 1 Sam 1:7; Esth 4:16; Jonah 3:5–7). Daniel's heart was so burdened for his people that it outweighed his hunger. As he prayed, Daniel also physically demonstrated humility and sorrow in the traditional way by covering himself with **sackcloth.** Often made of goat hair, this material was dark and rough. During times of mourning, the Israelites would remove their comfortable garments and clothe themselves in sackcloth (Gen 37:34; 2 Sam 3:31; 21:10; 1 Kgs 20:31–32). Additionally, Daniel placed **ashes** on himself, used as a reminder of destruction, death, and the deserved judgment of God (Job 2:8; Ezek 27:30; 28:18; Lam 3:16; Mal 4:3). The penitent repent in dust and ashes to confess that they are nothing before God (Gen 18:27), embracing God's chastisement, and acknowledging that they are undeserving of divine grace (Job 42:6; Jer 6:26). Unlike Israel fasting with sackcloth and ashes insincerely in the past (Isa 58:5), Daniel did so with his whole heart (cf. Jonah 3:6). By refusing food and donning funeral garb, Daniel demonstrated his humble and undistracted submission to the Lord in prayer.

James declared, "The effective prayer of a righteous man can accomplish much" (Jas 5:16). Ironically, the man who genuinely acknowledges his sin is considered righteous. Though James was speaking of the prophet Elijah, Daniel was also such a man. Daniel rested in God's sovereign providence (9:1) and placed his hope in the promises of Scripture (9:2). Daniel's prayer was characterized by humility, contrition, and godly sorrow for the sins of the nation. As the subsequent verses of Daniel 9 demonstrate, the Lord was pleased to hear and answer Daniel's prayer. Consequently, this prayer serves as a model worth emulating. When believers recognize God's sovereign providence, rest in Scripture's promises, and respond with supplication and penitence, expressing their need for grace, they can be confident that God will hear their prayers—answering them according to His perfect will. Such reality ought to strengthen the hearts of God's people with unwavering confidence and enduring comfort.

02

A PRAYER OF CONFESSION

DANIEL 9:4–14

And I prayed to Yahweh my God and confessed and said, "Alas, O Lord, the great and awesome God, who keeps His covenant and lovingkindness for those who love Him and keep His commandments, we have sinned and committed iniquity and acted wickedly and rebelled, even turning aside from Your commandments and judgments. Moreover, we have not listened to Your slaves the prophets, who spoke in Your name to our kings, our princes, our fathers, and all the people of the land.

To You, O Lord, belongs righteousness, but to us open shame, as it is this day—to the men of Judah, the inhabitants of Jerusalem, and all Israel, those who are nearby and those who are far away in all the countries to which You have banished them, because of their unfaithful deeds which they have committed against You. O Yahweh, to us belongs open shame, to our kings, our princes, and our fathers, because we have sinned against You. To the Lord our God *belong* compassion and forgiveness, for we have rebelled against Him; nor have we listened to the voice of Yahweh our God, to walk in His laws which He put before us through His slaves the prophets. Indeed all Israel has trespassed against Your law, even turning aside, not listening to Your voice; so the curse has been poured out on us, along with the oath which is written in the law of

Moses the servant of God, for we have sinned against Him. Thus He has established His words which He had spoken against us and against our judges who judged us, to bring on us great calamity; for under the whole heaven there has not been done *anything* like what was done to Jerusalem. As it is written in the law of Moses, all this calamity has come on us; yet we have not entreated the favor of Yahweh our God by turning from our iniquity and acting wisely in Your truth. Therefore Yahweh has watched over the calamity and brought it on us; for Yahweh our God is righteous with respect to all His deeds which He has done, but we have not listened to His voice."

The prophet Jeremiah revealed that God had decreed Israel's captivity to last for seventy years, after which He would bring His people back to their land (cf. Jer 25:11–12; 29:10). Daniel, who was more than eighty years old, had spent nearly all seventy of those years in exile in Babylon, so he was longing to see Jeremiah's prophecy fulfilled. Reading Jeremiah prompted him to pray that the Lord would fulfill His promise, keep the divinely promised timeline, and return the Israelites to the Promised Land.

Though Daniel knew that God is sovereign and that His perfect purposes cannot be thwarted, this confidence did not hinder him from praying. Rather, God's sovereignty compelled Daniel to cry out to the Lord to do what He had promised. The prophet petitioned God to bless Israel and to restore them to their homeland, showing them favor rather than judgment. Because Daniel knew from Scripture that this was the will of God, he boldly pled with the Lord to act. Even so, he realized that for Israel to be truly restored, the people needed to acknowledge their sin to God and walk in repentance. So Daniel, speaking for the sinful Israelites, focused his prayer on the admission of Israel's iniquity, attesting to the wickedness of the people and affirming the righteousness of Yahweh.

In his fervent petition, Daniel modeled a prayer of genuine repentance. He approached God with a humble attitude of contrition (vv. 4–6). He continued with a heartfelt acknowledgment of culpability (vv. 7–10). Then, he submitted to God with an honest acceptance of the consequences (vv. 11–14). Though it focused on Israel's sin, Daniel's prayer was ultimately hopeful because it rested confidently in the faithfulness, lovingkindness, and compassion of God. Prompted by Scripture and grounded in God's gracious character, Daniel's prayer demonstrated a heart of repentance earnestly seeking the glory of the Lord.

AN ATTITUDE OF CONTRITION

And I prayed to Yahweh my God and confessed and said, "Alas, O Lord, the great and awesome God, who keeps His covenant and lovingkindness for those who love Him and keep His commandments. We have sinned and committed iniquity and acted wickedly and rebelled, even turning aside from Your commandments and judgments. Moreover, we have not listened to Your slaves the prophets, who spoke in Your name to our kings, our princes, our fathers, and all the people of the land." (9:4–6)

Compelled by divine promise, Daniel **prayed to Yahweh** his **God.** Because Daniel **prayed** in repentance (cf. Ps 51:3–5; Luke 18:13), his request was characterized by humility and contrition. Unlike the self-righteous Pharisees of Jesus' day (cf. Luke 18:11–12), Daniel did not approach God with conceit or self-confidence, but with a sincere sense of the sinfulness and shame of his people. The answer to his prayer was completely dependent on the mercy and forgiveness of **Yahweh** his **God.** Appearing eight times in this book—every time in the context of a prayer from Daniel—the name **Yahweh** emphasizes God's covenant loyalty to Israel (cf. Exod 3:14–15). Because Daniel relied wholly on God's faithfulness, mercy, and lovingkindness, he addressed the Lord by using His covenant name,

Yahweh (Dan 9:8). In Exodus 34, the Lord revealed that His name reflected His immense grace, declaring, "Yahweh, Yahweh God, compassionate and gracious, slow to anger, and abounding in lovingkindness and truth; who keeps lovingkindness for thousands, who forgives iniquity, transgression, and sin" (Exod 34:6–7). Being the transcendent "I AM WHO I AM," He is faithful, never breaking His promise or covenant (cf. Gen 17:7; Deut 7:9; Titus 1:2). Daniel recognized the depth of Israel's sin, and therefore appealed to the Lord in light of His loyal and compassionate nature. Like the publican in Luke 18, Daniel exhibited humility and sorrow in including himself in the confession of the sins his people had committed (cf. Luke 18:13; 1 Tim 1:15). Not unlike the Son of God who carried the sins of His people, though Himself without sin, Daniel came to the Lord with devout love, calling Him **my God,** thereby conveying his personal affection and loyalty to Him.

In this intercessory prayer of repentance on behalf of his people, Daniel wholeheartedly **confessed** their sin. This term is consistently used in Scripture to denote the honest disclosure of one's wrongdoing (cf. Lev 5:5; 16:21; Num 5:7; Ezra 10:1; Neh 1:6; 9:2, 3). True repentance requires such confession (cf. Ps 51; 1 Chr 21; 1 John 1:9). Sinners cannot cling to wickedness while coming to God for grace (cf. Isa 55:7; Prov 28:13). In confessing sin, Daniel conformed not only to God's will but even to His plan. Long before, God had revealed through Moses that those in exile should confess their sins while the land recovered from missed sabbatical years (Lev 26:40–43). Having undoubtedly read this passage (cf. Dan 9:2), Daniel confessed his sin and the sin of his people.

The prophet's confession began by recounting God's character. With the word **alas,** Daniel uttered his deep distress at the offending sins against the holy and exalted Judge of heaven. Daniel knew that the **Lord** is the sovereign Master over all the nations (Dan 1:2), who had powerfully sustained His people in their captivity. Repeating this title (**Lord,** or Master) ten times in this prayer, Daniel emphasized his reliance on the sovereign will of **the great and awesome God.** His greatness is evidenced by His absolute perfection, infinite power, unfailing purposes, and unrivaled preeminence (cf. Deut 4:35). He is the **awesome God** whose might and majesty compel all to fear His name (cf. Ps 33:8).

While God is transcendent (enthroned above His creation), He is also immanent (engaging with His creatures) as He **keeps His covenant and lovingkindness for those who love Him and keep His commandments.** God is not only the omnipotent Ruler over the universe; He is also faithful and compassionate toward His people. Though Israel repeatedly violated His commands, He nonetheless kept **His covenant** with them, upholding every word of His promises without fail (cf. Deut 7:9, 12). God's faithfulness to Israel provided clear evidence of His **lovingkindness,** a term that denotes not only God's commitment to His people but also His mighty blessings in their lives. For this reason, the word is sometimes translated as "grace" in the New Testament (cf. John 1:17). On account of His loyal love, God delivered and preserved Israel throughout her history (cf. Ps 136). As Solomon professed, "O Yahweh, the God of Israel, there is no god like You in heaven above or upon earth beneath, keeping covenant and lovingkindness to Your slaves who walk before You with all their heart" (1 Kgs 8:23). Like Solomon, Daniel marveled not only at God's might but also at His grace.

Daniel also recognized God's justice, noting that divine blessing is reserved **for those who love Him and keep His commandments.** God does not merely desire that His people **keep His commandments,** carefully observing the precepts of His Word, but that such obedience be motivated by the fact that they **love Him.** True submission flows from love and affection to the Lord (cf. Deut 6:5; Matt 22:37; Mark 12:40; Luke 10:27; Eph 6:6). On the one hand, because Daniel was confessing sin, he acknowledged that his people had fallen short of God's righteous standard. They had failed to love the Lord wholeheartedly (cf. Deut 6:5). On the other hand, Daniel's confession was also a declaration of his desire for Israel to love God sincerely and live accordingly. Having acknowledged their sin, Daniel anchored his hope in God's lovingkindness, knowing the Lord stood ready to forgive and bless those who would approach Him in genuine repentance and faith.

Having affirmed both the greatness and grace of God, Daniel held nothing back as he began to recount Israel's sin. He used the plural pronoun **we** to include himself with his people as he interceded on their behalf. Though he was a trustworthy and obedient prophet who was mightily used by God, he was nonetheless acutely aware of his own sins (cf. Isa 6:5; Luke 5:8). In saying **"we,"** Daniel prayed both for himself and for his people. Like Paul who pleaded for God to work in the church (cf. Eph 3:14–19; Phil 1:9–11; Col 1:9–14), so Daniel implored the Lord on behalf of Israel. Throughout his prayer, Daniel constantly used the pronouns "we," "us," and "our," reflecting his humble identification with sinners and his sincere love for his people.

Daniel employed four verbs to describe the scope and severity of Israel's transgressions against God. He said, **"We have sinned," "committed iniquity," "acted wickedly,"** and **"rebelled." Sinned** is general for wrongdoing, including the idea of missing the mark (Judg 20:16), falling short of God's standard (cf. Rom 3:23), and deviating from His law (Deut 30:17; Ps 14:1–3; 53:1–3). Israel's sin, however, was not accidental or inadvertent but an intentional crime, as demonstrated by the verb **committed iniquity,** a term conveying the twistedness or perverseness of Israel's disobedience (cf. Hos 5:5; Mal 2:6). Daniel further expressed the depth of the nation's depravity with the verb **acted wickedly,** a word indicating guiltiness and condemnation before God (cf. Exod 22:9; Deut 25:1; 1 Kgs 8:32; Job 9:20). The final verb, **rebelled,** emphasizes that Israel's disobedience fundamentally reflected the nation's insubordination against God (Josh 1:18). By combining these four verbs to describe Israel's disobedience, Daniel articulated the extent and depth of the sinful corruption of his people.

Daniel expressed that Israel's wickedness manifested itself as Israel continued **turning aside from Your commandments and judgments.** Repentance is turning from sin and turning to God, but rebellion is the opposite—**turning aside** from God and His Word. Daniel admitted that his people had deliberately defected from God's **commandments and judgments** (cf. Isa 53:6). **Commandments** reflect the major principles of divine truth (Exod 20:1–17) while **judgments** refer to the particular and practical applications of those laws in any given situation. In some Old Testament passages, the phrase "commandments and judgments" is used with other terms such as "statutes" (Deut 8:11; 26:17; 1 Kgs 2:3) to emphasize the totality of God's law. When used by itself, the phrase conveys the most basic requirements of keeping God's law (1 Chr 28:7; Neh 9:29). As Daniel confessed, Israel had violated even the most rudimentary of God's requirements.

Daniel further acknowledged that Israel's rebellion was not occasional but perpetual. He confessed, **"Moreover, we have not listened to Your slaves the prophets, who spoke in Your name to our kings, our princes, our fathers, and all the people of the land."** Though God frequently commanded His people to heed divine revelation (cf. Deut 6:4; 30:11–14; Matt 17:5), the people had **not listened.** They refused to hear God's **slaves the prophets. Prophets** conveys the act of "calling out," and in describing them as **slaves,** Daniel reiterated that they submissively spoke what the Lord commanded them to declare. The prophets had the sacred honor of representing Yahweh and delivered His message to His people (cf. Deut 13; 18:18; Isa 6:8). Their proclamation confronted Israel's sin and called the people to repent (cf. Isa 1:18–20; Joel 2:12–13), giving them opportunity to respond accordingly (Ps 95:7–8; Isa 55:6; Heb 3:13–17; 2 Pet 3:9). But the nation paid no heed, refusing to turn from their wickedness and sin.

Israel stubbornly ignored the prophets, even though they ministered with divine authority as they

spoke in Your [Yahweh's] **name.** When a prophet spoke in God's name, he operated as God's herald, delivering a divinely inspired message backed by divinely inherent authority. To reject God's prophet was to reject the Holy One who sent him, an act of rebellion that warranted severe consequences (cf. Deut 13; 18:22). Israel's arrogant rejection of God's spokesmen pervaded every level of Israelite society: from every form of nobility (**our kings, our princes**) to the heads of families (**our fathers**) to every individual person (**all the people of the land**). They all heard the prophets' warnings and disregarded them (cf. Isa 65:2; Zech 7:13). So in his prayer, Daniel humbly confessed that Israel had sinned in the most egregious ways before the Lord (cf. Ps 32:1–3).

AN ACKNOWLEDGMENT
OF CULPABILITY

"**To You, O Lord, belongs righteousness, but to us open shame, as it is this day—to the men of Judah, the inhabitants of Jerusalem, and all Israel, those who are nearby and those who are far away in all the countries to which You have banished them, because of their unfaithful deeds which they have committed against You. O Yahweh, to us belongs open shame, to our kings, our princes, and our fathers, because we have sinned against You. To the**

Lord our God *belong* compassion and forgiveness, for we have rebelled against Him; nor have we listened to the voice of Yahweh our God, to walk in His laws which He put before us through His slaves the prophets." (9:7–10)

As Daniel continued to beseech the Lord in humble contrition, he moved from a general confession of his people's sin to a heartfelt acknowledgment of their shame and blameworthiness. Daniel began by establishing the stark difference between the rebellious Israelites and their righteous God. Drawing a contrast with the sinful nation, Daniel focused on the Lord and His blameless character saying, **"To You, O Lord, belongs righteousness."** Daniel's words emphasize two parallel realities: that God is **Lord** and Master over all peoples and nations, and that He runs and rules the universe in perfect **righteousness.** Whether God blesses, is patient with, or judges Israel or the nations (cf. Num 6:24; Joel 2:13; Ps 9:8), He always acts in perfect accord with His holy character. Daniel expressed this as a divine attribute by declaring that righteousness **belongs** to God. He is both its source and its standard, and there is no spot or stain of sin in Him (cf. Deut 32:4; 1 John 3:3).

In stark contrast, Daniel declared, **"but to us** [belongs] **open shame."** The prophet confessed that his people were full of **shame.** This word speaks not only of embarrassment but also of a deep sense of disgrace due to a dereliction of duty (Jer 14:4) and despicable behavior (Jer 6:15; Eph 5:12).

Because the nation's sin was flagrant and public, their shame was also **open** for all to see. Though sinners try to cover up their sin and shame (cf. Gen 3:7–8; Ps 32:3; Prov 28:13), Daniel confessed that Israel's shame was fully evident **as it is this day,** in Daniel's time. It was undeniable **to the men of Judah,** who like Daniel had been sent into exile (Dan 1:6; cf. Ezek 24:1–2; 33:21). **The inhabitants of Jerusalem,** the high nobles of the royal and priestly classes, also faced such humiliation. **All Israel,** both northern and southern kingdoms, could not escape the wrath of God. Daniel knew his people without exception had encountered God's chastisement, **those who** were **nearby and those who** were **far away in all the countries to which You** [God] **have banished them.** The Lord had warned that if Israel persisted in sin, they would be taken captive to enemy lands **nearby** or **far away** (1 Kgs 8:46; 2 Chr 6:36). God warned His people that He would **banish** them from their land if they did not repent (cf. Deut 30:1; Isa 8:22; 11:12; 27:13; 56:8; Jer 8:3; Ezek 4:13). But they had refused to listen.

Daniel confessed that Israel's disgrace was obvious **because of their unfaithful deeds which they have committed against You** [God]. **Unfaithful,** often used to describe adultery (Num 5:12, 27), conveyed that Israel had acted with the greatest infidelity and treachery against God. Daniel grasped the gravity of this sin **against** the Lord. In Hebrew, the phrase **which they have committed** repeats the word "unfaithful" (lit. "which they have committed in being *unfaithful*"), emphasizing the severity of Israel's spiritual adultery and corresponding shame.

Having exposed the depth of Israel's sin, Daniel then emphasized its breadth, saying, **"O Yahweh, to us belongs open shame, to our kings, our princes, and our fathers, because we have sinned against You."** These words declared that Israel's crimes were committed against **Yahweh,** who had chosen them and entered into a covenant relationship with them (Exod 19:5–6; Ps 51:4). In opening this line with a breathtaking **"O Yahweh,"** Daniel conveyed the emotion of the disgrace in Israel's iniquity. **Yahweh** had given this people His personal name and precious covenant promises, yet they responded with rebellion. Accordingly, Daniel acknowledged that the **open shame** of humiliating exile was fully deserved (**to us** it **belongs**). The entire nation—from Israel's highest royalty (**kings**) to its nobility (**princes**) to every family unit (**fathers**)—deserved the full weight of divine discipline. That Daniel spoke of a plurality of **our kings, our princes, and our fathers** indicates that Israel's disobedience was systemic—pervading multiple social classes and successive generations. Daniel declared that God's chosen people had flagrantly **sinned against** the Lord (Pss 14:1–3; 53:1–3).

In stark contrast to Israel's treachery against God, Daniel declared that **"to the Lord our God *belong* compassion and forgiveness."** Israel had no love for God, while God had **compassion** for His own, caring for them as a mother cares for her children (cf. 1 Kgs 3:26). God also extended **forgiveness** to His people. This particular Hebrew term translated **forgiveness** describes the kind of pardon God alone can offer (cf. Exod 34:9; Pss 25:11; 103:3). While a person is not to hold a sin against another, God alone is able to forgive transgression and declare the sinner to be right with Him. Only the Lord can remove the sin as far as the east is from the west (Ps 103:12), so that the condemned criminal might be pardoned and received as God's own child (cf. Rom 5:10). By referring to Yahweh as **the Lord our God,** Daniel recognized God's immense patience with Israel, since He still had a relationship with His chosen people despite their disobedience. Both words **compassion** and **forgiveness** are plural in Hebrew, emphasizing God's abundant kindness.

The richness of God's compassion and forgiveness was repeatedly seen in the midst of Israel's persistent disobedience. As Daniel confessed, **"for we have rebelled against Him; nor have we listened to the voice of Yahweh our God, to walk in His laws which**

He put before us through His slaves the prophets."
God's longsuffering was clearly manifested in Daniel's
comprehensive confession that **we**—the nation of
Israel throughout the generations—**rebelled against**
God and committed treason against Him (cf. Dan 9:5;
Judg 2:18–19). Israel defied God by refusing to heed
His prophets (Dan 9:6) through whom **the voice of
Yahweh our God** was revealed. To listen to the Lord
is to yield to His Word, acknowledging His supremacy
and submitting to His commands (Mic 6:8). Listening
is foundational to honoring God, so it is frequently
emphasized in the Old Testament (e.g., Deut 6:4; Isa
55:2). That Israel refused to obey **Yahweh our God**
was especially heinous since they, His covenant people,
had pledged their obedience to Him (Exod 24:7).

This resistance to God further manifested itself
in Israel's life as they refused to **walk in His laws.**
Even though God **put** His law **before** His people
through the constant and faithful proclamation
of **His slaves the prophets,** Israel was unmoved
and persisted in obstinate disobedience. Yet, in spite
of such comprehensive and unceasing rebellion,
the Lord still responded to Israel with forbearance
and lovingkindness.

Daniel acknowledged that God was not only
righteous (Dan 9:5) but also gracious. He was faithful
to His covenant promise, extending compassion upon
His people and forgiving them when they repented.

Such uprightness and mercy stood in stark contrast to the sinfulness and shame of Israel. In response, Daniel eagerly proclaimed Yahweh's righteousness and grace, demonstrating that true confession gives glory to God (cf. Josh 7:19).

AN ACCEPTANCE OF
THE CONSEQUENCES

"Indeed all Israel has trespassed against Your law, even turning aside, not listening to Your voice; so the curse has been poured out on us, along with the oath which is written in the law of Moses the servant of God, for we have sinned against Him. Thus He has established His words which He had spoken against us and against our judges who judged us, to bring on us great calamity; for under the whole heaven there has not been done *anything* like what was done to Jerusalem. As it is written in the law of Moses, all this calamity has come on us; yet we have not entreated the favor of Yahweh our God by turning from our iniquity and acting wisely in Your truth. Therefore Yahweh has watched over the calamity and brought it on us; for Yahweh our God is righteous with respect to all His deeds which He has done, but we have not listened to His voice." (9:11–14)

Unlike Cain who protested God's punishment (Gen 4:13), Daniel remained resolute that God was absolutely just, saying, **"Indeed all Israel has trespassed against Your law, even turning aside, not listening to Your voice."** Daniel reiterated that Israel had defected from the Lord, **even turning aside** to worship other gods. They rejected His Word by **not listening to Your** [God's] **voice.** In sum, **all Israel has trespassed against Your law. Trespassed** denotes going beyond a set limit or crossing over a marked boundary (cf. Gen 18:5; Deut 4:14; Dan 11:10, 20, 40). God's people had violated the parameters of God's **law,** straying off course and trampling on His holy standards.

Daniel acknowledged that nothing less than **the curse** of God's wrath (Deut 28:15), which He vowed to execute against the wicked (Gen 24:41; 26:28; Lev 5:1; Num 5:21), **has been poured out on us** [Israel]. This violent, unrelenting, and devastating fury was **poured out** like an overwhelming torrent of rain (cf. Exod 9:33; 2 Sam 21:10). The fall of Jerusalem and the resulting exile were the evidence of this divine judgment (cf. 2 Kgs 25:1–21). To be certain, God had warned His people about their pending punishment. His curse was preceded by His **oath which is written in the law of Moses the servant of God** to deal with sin. His warning was clearly preserved in the **written** declarations found **in the law of Moses the servant**

of God. Israel could not accuse the Lord of unfairness because their punishment was warranted and prescribed. They could not plead ignorance since they had been duly warned by Moses and the prophets. As Daniel emphatically lamented, **"for we have sinned against Him."**

After acknowledging again that Israel was responsible, Daniel declared, **"Thus He has established His words which He had spoken against us and against our judges who judged us."** God, by acting justly, had **established** the integrity of **His words.** Unlike the people who did not keep God's Word, the Lord upheld His covenant and promises without fail. His actions were righteous since **He had spoken** those words **against us.** At Sinai (Exod 19:16–24) and on the Plains of Moab (Deut 29:1), God told Israel what He would do against them for their sin, and Israel agreed to those terms. At that time, the Lord spoke **against our** [Israel's] **judges who judged us,** those who rendered legal decisions (1:16; 16:18; 19:17) and implemented them (Num 25:5; Judg 2:16). As those who **judged** Israel according to God's law, these rulers not only knew the law but were to employ it to condemn the guilty. Therefore, they could hardly object when God applied the same standard to them.

Daniel affirmed that God was vindicated in whatever He did, even **to bring on us great calamity. Calamity** conveys the harm of God's punishment against His people. The injury inflicted upon Israel was so **great** that it overwhelmed and scattered the nation with such severity that Daniel explained, **"For under the whole heaven there has not been done anything like what was done to Jerusalem."** Daniel declared that **what was done to Jerusalem** had no parallel in time (**there has not been done *anything***) and space (**under the whole heaven**). While Babylon had destroyed many cities, Jerusalem's destruction was unique because it marked God's abandonment of His people (cf. Ezek 9:3; 10:1–4; 10:18–19; 11:22–23). Just as God's deliverance of His people *from* another nation—Egypt—was unparalleled (cf. Deut 4:34), so was the deliverance of His people *to* another nation—Babylon—unmatched (cf. 28:68). As Moses had warned generations earlier, "It will be that as Yahweh delighted over you to prosper you and multiply you, so Yahweh will delight over you to make you perish and destroy you; and you will be torn from the land where you are entering to possess it" (28:63). Israel uniquely knew what it meant to be graciously chosen and justly chastened.

Daniel also confessed that God was justified not merely in the past but also in the present, declaring, **"As it is written in the law of Moses, all this calamity has come on us; yet we have not entreated the favor of Yahweh our God by turning from our iniquity and acting wisely in Your truth."** Daniel moved from Israel's past to her present. He recounted that **this** recent **calamity,** God's terrible judgment against Jerusalem (Dan 9:12), took place according to God's sovereign purposes, since it was prophesied long beforehand, being **written in the law of Moses.**

Daniel again acknowledged Israel's continued reluctance to repent, affirming that **we** [Israel] **have not entreated the favor of Yahweh our God by turning from our iniquity and acting wisely in Your truth.** The word **entreated** literally means "to be sick" (cf. Gen 48:1; Deut 29:22; Judg 16:7), conveying one's distress over sin and utter dependence on God's **favor** (cf. Ps 32:3–4; Isa 53:4–5, 10). Daniel knew that with the Lord there is such kindness because **Yahweh** is the covenant God characterized by faithfulness, forgiveness, lovingkindness, and truth (Exod 34:6–7).

Daniel also declared that Yahweh was **our** (Israel's) **God** who had chosen Israel to be His people. Yet, Israel remained recalcitrant. They showed no remorse for their sin. If the people had been genuinely repentant, they would have repudiated their sin, **turning from** their **iniquity.** They would have begun to walk in obedience, **acting wisely in** God's **truth.** The Hebrew word for **acting wisely** refers to the skillful application of divine truth to everyday life (cf. Deut 29:9; 32:29; Josh 1:7; 1 Sam 18:30). The fruit of repentance is not merely minimal obedience but wholehearted devotion to living out the **truth** of

God's Word (cf. Deut 6:5; Luke 9:23; 2 Cor 7:10–11). True repentance includes both **turning from** one's **iniquity and acting wisely in** God's **truth.** Tragically, Israel had done neither. The people knew what to do but they still did not do it. Thus, they deserved the punishment they received.

Because Israel remained unrepentant, Daniel declared, **"Therefore Yahweh has watched over the calamity and brought it on us."** That **Yahweh has watched over the calamity** speaks to His effective sovereignty. Just as God was watchful over His Word to do it (Jer 1:12), so **Yahweh has watched over the calamity,** attentive and active, to ensure it came to pass. Nothing could slip by the Lord nor thwart or withstand His powerful control. So Daniel declared that God, exercising His sovereign authority, **brought** this just judgment **on us,** the generation of Daniel. In submission to God's will, Daniel acknowledged, **"Yahweh our God is righteous with respect to all His deeds which He has done, but we have not listened to His voice,"** again affirming that God was exclusively right (cf. Dan 9:7) and Israel was entirely wrong (cf. 9:6, 10, 11), both in the past and in Daniel's day (9:11–13). The prophet's final words summarized the point of his prayer and the nature of true confession. True confession declares not only that the sinner is guilty but also that he fully accepts responsibility for the deserved punishment.

The people of Israel, throughout their history, often hypocritically honored God with their lips but their hearts were far from Him (Isa 29:13). But Daniel's prayer was expressed from lips that were moved by a heart after God's own (cf. 1 Sam 13:14; Acts 13:22). In his confession, Daniel displayed a humble approach, a heartfelt acknowledgment, and an honest assessment of Israel's sin and its consequences. His prayer of repentance exhibited an attitude of contrition, an acknowledgment of culpability, and an acceptance of the consequences. Daniel did not make excuses or refuse God's discipline but embraced it, recognizing that he and his nation were deserving of it all. Such genuine confession was for God's glory (cf. Dan 9:20).

03

A PRAYER OF PETITION

DANIEL 9:15–19

"So now, O Lord our God, who have brought Your people out of the land of Egypt with a strong hand and have made a name for Yourself, as it is this day—we have sinned; we have acted wickedly. O Lord, in accordance with all Your righteousness, let now Your anger and Your wrath turn away from Your city Jerusalem, Your holy mountain; for because of our sins and the iniquities of our fathers, Jerusalem and Your people *have become* a reproach to all those around us. So now, our God, listen to the prayer of Your slave and to his supplications, and for Your sake, O Lord, let Your face shine on Your desolate sanctuary. O my God, incline Your ear and listen! Open Your eyes and see our desolations and the city which is called by Your name; for we are not presenting our supplications before You on account of *any* righteousness of our own, but on account of Your abundant compassion. O Lord, listen! O Lord, forgive! O Lord, give heed and take action! For Your own sake, O my God, do not delay, because Your city and Your people are called by Your name."

The Lord Jesus gave His followers a powerful promise about prayer: "Whatever you ask in My name, this will I do, so that the Father may be glorified in the Son" (cf. John 14:13; 1 John 5:14). But James warned that many ask and do not receive because they ask with wrong motives, selfishly desiring that God satisfy their pleasures (Jas 4:3). Such people do not petition the Father in Jesus' name, according to His will. The fundamental function of prayer is to align the will of the believer with the will of God—to submit to God's plan, power, and purposes. Even as the Lord Jesus Himself prayed in the Garden of Gethsemane, "Yet not as I will, but as You will" (Matt 26:39).

The final portion of Daniel's prayer contains his petition, exemplifying a heart that makes requests according to God's name. Because Daniel studied the Scriptures, he knew the will of God and aligned himself with it. Daniel petitioned the Lord to fulfill the promises He had made to Israel in His Word. Daniel understood from the Law of Moses that God's judgment of Israel was a fulfillment of His warnings to the people (Dan 9:11; cf. Deut 27–28). He also knew from the prophecies of Jeremiah that God would restore the nation of Israel (Dan 9:2; Jer 25:10–11; 29:10; 32:42). Informed by biblical truth, Daniel petitioned God to end His people's chastening in exile. They had suffered nearly seventy years in a foreign land under the oppression of pagan kings. Daniel acknowledged that this captivity was God's discipline of Israel for their rebellion against the covenant that God had made with them. As this judgment was nearing its end, Daniel prayed for the nation's forgiveness and restoration in keeping with God's plan.

In pleading for God to forgive and restore Israel, Daniel prayed not only according to God's will but also for His glory. He sought the restoration of Israel so that God's name might be magnified in Israel and among the nations. In honoring God's righteousness (vv. 15–16), His relationship (vv. 17–18), and His renown (v. 19), Daniel modeled the way true prayer honors God in its petitions.

HONORING GOD'S RIGHTEOUSNESS

"So now, O Lord our God, who have brought Your people out of the land of Egypt with a strong hand and have made a name for Yourself, as it is this day— we have sinned; we have acted wickedly. O Lord, in accordance with all Your righteousness, let now Your anger and Your wrath turn away from Your city Jerusalem, Your holy mountain; for because of our sins and the iniquities of our fathers, Jerusalem and Your people *have become* a reproach to all those around us." (9:15–16)

With the words **so now,** Daniel turned from confession to petition. Though making a request of God, Daniel's prayer focused not on himself but on his Sovereign, calling Him the **Lord our God.** The term

Lord is not God's covenant name (Yahweh) but the title meaning "master" (*Adonai*), emphasizing His total dominion over all peoples and events. This is the fifth time Daniel used this title for God in his prayer (vv. 3, 4, 7, 9) as he constantly worshiped God and submitted to His control. In the same way that the Lord Jesus commanded the saints to pray according to His will (John 14:13; cf. 1 John 5:14), so Daniel appealed to God to enact His sovereign plan. By calling Him **our God,** Daniel also petitioned God based on His great love and commitment for His chosen people.

Daniel declared that God's sovereign will and commitment to His people was demonstrated as the Lord had **brought Your** [His] **people out of the land of Egypt with a strong hand.** The Exodus demonstrated God's loyalty to Israel and established them as His **people.** The Exodus also exhibited that God's power was unstoppable as He delivered His people **out of the land of Egypt,** a world superpower, doing so **with a strong hand.** The devastating miracles (Exod 6:1; 13:3) that broke the hardened will of Pharaoh (3:19) showcased to the watching world God's preeminent power to save.

As Daniel recounted, because of the Exodus, the Lord God **made a name for Yourself** [Himself]. A **name** is not merely a title but a reference to one's character and reputation (Exod 20:7; Prov 22:1; Eccl 7:1). The Exodus demonstrated the transcendent nature of God before all the nations (Exod 9:16; 15:14; 18:1; 2 Chr 20:29). This is one of the reasons the book of Exodus is appropriately called the book of "names" in Hebrew, since it revealed the fullness of the name and the nature of God. The Exodus demonstrated to Israel and the world that God is Yahweh, the covenant keeping God of grace (Exod 34:6–8), the supreme God of all power (18:1), and the Lord and Master over all people (15:17). God's reputation, which dramatically reverberated throughout the world in the days of Moses (Exod 18:1; cf. Josh 9), continued **as it is this day,** to the time of Daniel. God's character has been clearly seen in subsequent history, as He preserved His people through the wilderness (Neh 9:19–21), empowered them to conquer the Promised Land (Josh 23:3), rescued them from the Philistines (1 Sam 7:10), and delivered them from dangers throughout the centuries (Ps 136:10–24). Daniel knew that God had established and protected His name (Exod 9:16; 20:7; Deut 5:11; 2 Sam 7:23), so that the nations would fear Him (1 Sam 5:7–8). Daniel revered God's name, affirming the truth revealed by God to Malachi: "My name *will be* great among the nations, and in every place incense is going to be presented to My name, as well as a grain offering *that is* clean; for My name will be great among the nations" (Mal 1:11).

Out of concern for God's name, Daniel confessed, **"We have sinned; we have acted**

wickedly," acknowledging that Israel had **sinned** against God and violated their covenant with Him. In saying that they had **acted wickedly,** Daniel admitted that the people's actions indicted them of guilt. They deserved to receive God's displeasure and discipline. Any appeal on Israel's behalf was not grounded in self-righteousness or human merit, but only in the mercy and grace of God. Accordingly, all glory would go to God for the mercy and compassion He demonstrated to His people.

Because of Israel's unworthiness, Daniel appealed to God based upon His character, praying to the **Lord in accordance with all Your** [God's] **righteousness.** In addressing Yahweh as **Lord** (*Adonai*), Daniel turned to the Master who possessed the sovereign power to act. Having read the Scriptures (cf. Dan 9:2, 11), Daniel knew that though Israel would sin and be exiled, God would keep His covenant and bring the people back to their land (cf. Deut 4:25–31; Ezek 11:17). Daniel had even read that God would intervene after seventy years of captivity in Babylon (Jer 25:11–12; cf. 29:10). Pleading with the **Lord,** Daniel urged Him that the time had come for His will to be done. Likewise, he petitioned the Lord to act **in accordance with all Your** [His] **righteousness,** knowing that the **all** holy and **righteous** God would certainly uphold His covenant promises.

To put God's unfailing righteousness on display, Daniel entreated the Lord, **"Let now Your anger and Your wrath turn away from Your city Jerusalem, Your holy mountain."** God's **anger** emphasizes His severe attitude against His people while His **wrath** refers to His destructive actions to punish rebellious Israel. The pairing of these words conveyed the magnitude of God's fury, as evidenced in His judgment against Sodom and Gomorrah (Deut 29:23), the idolatrous Israelites who worshipped the golden calf (9:19), and also the city of Jerusalem (Jer 32:31). In Israel's exile in 586 BC, God's anger and wrath made Judah and the streets of its capital a waste place (Jer 44:6; Lam 4:11; Ezek 5:13). But just as God had dispensed judgment on Jerusalem, so He promised to turn that fury away and return His people to that very place (Jer 32:37). Daniel asked the Lord to act on that promise, especially since Israel's capital was **Your city Jerusalem, Your holy mountain.** Jerusalem was God's (**Your**) **city,** the place where He had committed His glory and name (cf. Deut 12:5; Ps 132:13–14). It was also His (**Your**) **holy mountain,** the place where He will one day be worshiped by the whole world (Isa 11:9; 27:13; 56:7; Ezek 20:40; Zech 8:3). As with His justice, in restraining wrath and showing mercy, God would be magnified in His righteousness as He fulfilled His promises, kept His commitments, and upheld His purposes for the world.

Daniel understood that this divine mercy was required and urgent. He explained that **"because of our** [Israel's] **sins and the iniquities of our fathers, Jerusalem and Your people *have become* a reproach to all those around us."** Though emphasizing the ruinous state of Jerusalem, Daniel maintained the culpability of his people, saying, **"Because of our sins and the iniquities of our fathers."** In acknowledging their responsibility, Daniel identified first **our sins** and only then impugned **the iniquities** and transgressions **of our fathers.** As the nation was justly punished, Daniel reported that **Jerusalem and Your** [God's] **people *have become* a reproach to all those around us.** The city of **Jerusalem** had been left in ruins when it was sacked in 586 BC, and the **people** had become a disgrace as they were scattered in exile. Jerusalem and its former inhabitants became **a reproach to all those around** Israel. Daniel was repulsed by the ridicule God received from the enemies of His people. The praying prophet's attitude was similar to that of David who proclaimed: "For zeal for Your house has consumed me, and the reproaches of those who reproach You have fallen on me" (Ps 69:9). So Daniel begged the Lord to intervene, not for Israel's sake but for the sake of His reputation: so that the reproaches of the enemy would end and God's glorious name would be magnified.

HONORING GOD'S RELATIONSHIP

"So now, our God, listen to the prayer of Your slave and to his supplications, and for Your sake, O Lord, let Your face shine on Your desolate sanctuary. O my God, incline Your ear and listen! Open Your eyes and see our desolations and the city which is called by Your name; for we are not presenting our supplications before You on account of *any* righteousness of our own, but on account of Your abundant compassion." (9:17–18)

With another **so now** (cf. Dan 9:15), Daniel moved from appealing to God's righteousness to His relationship with His people, addressing the Lord as **our God.** Daniel's humility was again evident as he pled with the Lord to **listen to the prayer of Your** [God's] **slave**—a reference to his lowly condition and total submission to his heavenly Master. Putting away every hint of pride, Daniel recognized his dependence on God's grace as he made **his supplications** to the Lord. Since **supplications** has at its Hebrew root the word "grace," Daniel was putting himself at the mercy of God's grace (cf. Heb 4:16).

Though Daniel prayed for his people to receive mercy, his focus was ultimately fixed on the glory of God as his petitions were **for Your sake, O Lord.** Once again, Daniel called God **"Lord,"** emphasizing

His universal rule (Ps 110:4; cf. 24:1; 47:7–8) and plan to restore Israel (Ezek 39:25–29) and to be worshiped in the holy city (Isa 2:2–3; Zech 1:16; 12:6).

Intent on seeing God honored, Daniel asked, **"Let Your face shine on Your desolate sanctuary."** The expression **"let Your face shine"** describes God looking favorably on His people and graciously restoring them to their homeland (cf. Pss 31:16; 80:3, 7, 19). Recalling the Aaronic blessing (Num 6:25), Daniel pleaded with God to fulfill His promise to bless His people and break through the darkness of their exile (cf. Isa 9:2; Jer 32:41–42). Then, God's (**Your**) **desolate sanctuary,** an unusable ruin and symbol of Israel's anguish (Dan 8:13; 9:26; 11:31), would be majestically restored (Ezek 40–48; Zech 2:4–5; 6:13). **Sanctuary** literally means "holy place," the pinnacle of God's holy mountain (cf. Dan 9:16) from which His glory will shine before the nations. Daniel viewed the rebuilding of the Lord's sanctuary as a masterpiece of God's love and loyalty to His people, a place where He would ultimately be worshiped by all the nations.

With the cry **"O my God,"** Daniel reiterated the intimacy of his relationship with the Lord and the urgency of his plea. Daniel passionately asked the Lord to **incline** His **ear and listen** as well as to **open** His **eyes and see.** He desired the Lord to engage fully with his prayer and to intervene. The petitioning prophet begged the Lord to pay the fullest attention to Israel's

desolations and the city which is called by His **name.** Not only was the sanctuary desolate (cf. Dan 9:16) but the people were also suffering (cf. Deut 28:15–68). Like the sanctuary, the people languished in scattered shame. Daniel petitioned God to look upon their devastation and have pity.

Daniel further pointed out to the Lord that **the city which is called by Your name** lay in ruins. God had frequently declared that He had associated His **name** and reputation with the **city** of Jerusalem (cf. 2 Kgs 21:7; 2 Chr 7:16; 32:3; 33:4). Because His fame was linked with Israel's capital, God defended it in the past (2 Kgs 19:23–28). His reputation was associated with the majesty of the city (cf. 1 Kgs 10:2, 9). As Solomon prayed:

> Also concerning the foreigner who is not of Your people Israel, if he comes from a far country for Your name's sake (for they will hear of Your great name and Your strong hand, and of Your outstretched arm); so if he comes and prays toward this house, listen in heaven Your dwelling place, and do according to all for which the foreigner calls to You, in order that all the peoples of the earth may know Your name to fear You, as *do* Your people Israel, and to know that Your name is called upon this house which I have built. (1 Kgs 8:41–43)

In emphasizing that Jerusalem was called by Yahweh's **name,** Daniel showed that his fervency was not for himself but for God's honor. Daniel recoiled at the notion that Israel's situation would blemish God's reputation among the nations. Because Daniel was so burdened for God's glory, he urged the Lord to act.

To affirm further that his singular passion was the glory of God (cf. Dan 2:23, 28; Ps 27:4), Daniel reiterated that **we** [Israel] **are not presenting our supplications before You** [God] **on account of *any* righteousness of our own.** The word **presenting** means "to fall," emphasizing that Daniel humbly laid his requests **before** God to accept or reject. Dependent on God's grace (**supplications**) and submitting to His authority, Daniel focused entirely on the Lord, knowing that it was **not on account of *any* righteousness of** their **own.** Daniel had confessed that he and his people were guilty and that God alone was righteous (Dan 9:7–10).

Having reiterated his low view of self and his exalted view of God, Daniel revealed his true motivation in petitioning for the temple. It was not due to a sense of entitlement but **on account of Your** [God's] **abundant compassion.** The term **compassion** is often used for a mother's love for her child (Isa 49:15), the profound empathy a father has for his own (Ps 103:13), and the compelling sense of care one has for the helpless (Jer 6:23). While false gods can show no care nor offer forgiveness for their people (cf. Pss 115:4–7; 135:15–18), God has true affection for His own in **abundance.** Though He had temporarily removed His compassion to judge His people (Isa 9:17; Hos 2:4), He promised to return His mercy and grace with great abundance (cf. Isa 49:13; 54:7; Jer 12:15). In 1 Kings 8:50, the Lord specifically promised that if His people prayed toward Jerusalem in exile, He would rekindle such compassion towards them. Having read the Scripture (Dan 9:2, 11; Jer 29:10), Daniel knew exactly what to pray, not only petitioning according to God's will but also zealously seeking God's glory in bestowing His people with abundant compassion.

HONORING GOD'S RENOWN

"O Lord, listen! O Lord, forgive! O Lord, give heed and take action! For Your own sake, O my God, do not delay, because Your city and Your people are called by Your name." (9:19)

Daniel's petition culminated with an emotive cry of fervent faith to the Master who reigns over all: **"O Lord."** Daniel's prayer not only conformed to God's sovereignty but also expressed great confidence in light of it (Heb 4:16). Israel's God was not impotent like the gods of the nations who had eyes that could not see and ears that could not hear (Pss 115:5–7; 135:15–18). Daniel pled with the Lord because he knew that the one true God would see, hear, and act.

In concluding his intercession, Daniel first cried out for the Lord to listen to his request, an appeal he had already made (Dan 9:17–18). Knowing that God was not obligated to answer someone as unworthy as him (9:9–10), Daniel nonetheless pleaded with the Lord to consider his request.

Daniel's second and central petition was for the Lord to **forgive.** While he had already asked God to **listen** (9:17–18) and to act on his prayer (9:16–18), he now asked God to **forgive,** to grant a pardon to His people. Though believers must not hold sin against others, only God is able to atone for sin (Isa 53:5–6; Acts 4:12; 1 Tim 2:5–6), remove it as far as the east is from the west (Ps 103:12), and reconcile the sinner to Himself (cf. Job 14:15). God alone can offer the remission of sins (Heb 9:26). Fully aware of the gravity of sin, Daniel knew that what he and his people needed was not merely physical deliverance but spiritual forgiveness. Daniel understood that the only way God would listen and act was if He first pardoned Israel. He recognized that, for sinners, there is no greater need than God's forgiveness (cf. Isa 59:1–2; Ps 32:1–2).

Only when God forgave would He do the third of Daniel's requests: **give heed and take action.** Daniel desired for God to **give heed,** or carefully survey His reproach in the suffering of His people and the devastation of His city (Dan 9:18), and then **take**

action to restore the Lord's city (vv. 16, 18), sanctuary (v. 17), and people (vv. 18, 19).

Daniel reiterated that his humble appeals were **for Your** [God's] **own sake.** Throughout his entire confession, Daniel was consumed with honoring the Lord by confessing God's righteousness (vv. 7–9) and relationship (vv. 15–18). The prophet fixed his attention on God to the end of his prayer, demonstrating that his heart was completely united in zeal for the Lord (Ps 86:10). For Daniel, God was not a distant being in heaven, but **my God,** the God whom Daniel personally loved and whose glory he sought.

The prophet desired for God to take action and **not delay, because Your** [God's] **city and Your people are called by Your name.** Yahweh was known as the God of Israel (Gen 33:20; Deut 7:6; Ps 135:4; Judg 20:2; 2 Sam 14:13; Zech 2:8) and His reputation was inextricably linked with Jerusalem (1 Kgs 8:41–42; 2 Chr 7:16). Daniel detested the idea of hearing God's enemies use His **city and people** to defame His name (cf. Ezek 36:20–21). Knowing that God had glorified Himself in judgment (cf. Exod 9:16; 14:4; Ps 96:10–13; Isa 2:11; Rom 9:17), Daniel looked to Scripture and discerned that the time had come for God to be magnified in His mercy toward Israel (Jer 29:10). Because Daniel could not bear seeing God's name reproached, he urged God to **not delay** so that He would be honored (Pss 29:2; 86:9).

Scripture declares that people often pray with false motives, asking God for what would be spent on the pleasures of this world (Jas 4:3). Daniel, in contrast, was concerned not for himself but for the glory of his Lord. He prayed for God's will and not his own (cf. Ps 115:1; Matt 26:39), illustrating what it means to pray in the name of the Lord, consistent with the Lord's character (cf. John 14:14; 1 John 5:14). For Daniel, prayer was an act of submission to the will of God, informed by the Word of God, and focused on the worship of God. In this way, his prayer provides a powerful model for believers to emulate in any generation.

04

THE SEVENTY WEEKS

DANIEL 9:20–27

Now while I was speaking and praying, and confessing my sin and the sin of my people Israel, and presenting my supplication before Yahweh my God in behalf of the holy mountain of my God, and while I was still speaking in prayer, then the man Gabriel, whom I had seen in the vision previously, touched me in *my* extreme weariness about the time of the evening offering. Then he made *me* understand and spoke with me and said, "O Daniel, I have now come forth to give you insight with understanding. At the beginning of your supplications the word was issued, so I have come to tell *you*, for you are highly esteemed; so understand the message and gain understanding in what has appeared. Seventy weeks have been determined for your people and for your holy city, to finish the transgression, to make an end of sin, to make atonement for iniquity, to bring in everlasting righteousness, to seal up vision and prophecy, and to anoint *the* Holy of Holies. So you are to know and have insight *that* from the going out of a word to restore and rebuild Jerusalem until Messiah the Prince, *there will be* seven weeks and sixty-two weeks; it will be restored and rebuilt, with plaza and moat, even in times of distress. Then after the sixty-two weeks the Messiah will be cut off and have nothing, and the people of the prince who is to come will destroy the city and the sanctuary. And its end *will come* with a flood; even to the end there will be war; desolations are decreed. And he will make a firm covenant with the many for one week, but in the middle of the week he will make sacrifice and grain offering cease; and on the wing of abominations *will come* one who makes desolate, even until a complete destruction, one that is decreed, is poured out on the one who makes desolate."

The Old Testament abounds with divine prophecies in which the Lord revealed precise details about events that were yet future. Years before they took place, God foretold the coming Exodus (Gen 15:13–14), the conquest of Canaan (15:16), and the exile into captivity (Deut 28:64; Isa 5:26–30; Hos 7:11). The prophets even identified individuals by name long before they were born, such as Josiah (1 Kgs 13:2) and Cyrus (Isa 45:1), describing their significant roles in God's plan for His people. Daniel, in similar fashion, disclosed the flow of history as God revealed it to him, detailing the rise and fall of Babylon, Medo-Persia, Greece, Rome, and even the revived Roman Empire under the rule of the Antichrist (cf. Dan 2:36–45; 7:1–8; 11:1–45).

Though the Old Testament contains many predictive passages, with several themes, its primary prophetic focus centers on the coming Messiah, who is identified by various names, titles, and descriptives that depict

His nature and anticipate His work. He is the Anointed One (Ps 2:2); the Branch (Zech 3:8); the Captain (Josh 5:4); and the Prince of Peace (Isa 9:6). He is the Stone the builders rejected (Ps 118:22); the Suffering Servant who would die for His people (Isa 53); the One pierced for sinners (Zech 12:10); and the Holy One who would not see corruption on account of His resurrection (Ps 16:10). He is the Horn of Salvation (18:2); the Fountain of cleansing (Zech 13:1); the One who will justify the many (Isa 53:11); and the Seed who will reverse the curse (Gen 3:15; Gal 3:16). As the prophets declared, the Messiah will achieve such cosmic victory because He is the Son of God (Ps 2:7, 12); Immanuel, God with us (Isa 7:14); the Glory of God (60:1); the Mighty God (9:6); and the King, Yahweh of Hosts (Isa 6:5; John 12:41).

Old Testament prophecy provides a powerful testimony to the divine authorship and veracity of Scripture. Its astounding precision attests to God's sovereign omniscience, demonstrating that He knows and ordains the future, thus reigning in absolute sovereignty over history. These prophecies, being perfectly fulfilled, confirm that the Bible is the revealed Word of God. Scripture is the prophetic Word, as Peter declared, which is more sure than human opinion or experience (2 Pet 1:19). Because it is the very Word of God (2 Tim 3:16), it not only discloses the truth but also dictates it, declaring both that which is and that which is to come.

While God revealed much through future prophecies, He did not unveil all. Moses acknowledged that "The secret things belong to Yahweh" (Deut 29:29). Peter also confessed that the prophets generally did not possess full knowledge concerning "what time or what kind of time" their predictions would take place (1 Pet 1:11). They knew of the "sufferings of Christ and the glories to follow," but they did not know exactly when or how those details would be fulfilled.

Prior to Daniel 9, the Lord had not detailed the chronology of future history. As a result, Daniel's seventy-week prophecy is unique and epic. With Israel being in exile nearly seven decades, Daniel was eager for the nation's physical and spiritual restoration. The prophet had no doubt that God's promise of salvation for the nation would be realized at the end of the Babylonian exile. However, the Lord revealed that His plans for Israel would reach into the distant future, encompassing a period of seventy weeks, that is seventy times seven years. Through Daniel, the Lord provided a timeline for the major events Israel would experience from the days of Daniel to the end of history. In this remarkable revelation, God outlined a precise chronology regarding when Christ would die to accomplish redemption (Dan 9:25–26), and the Antichrist would rise and reign before finally being destroyed at the return of Christ (v. 27).

God revealed that 490 years were determined for Israel, during which Israel would be at the center of God's redemptive plan, culminating in Israel's ultimate restoration and salvation (cf. Rom 11:26). In verses 20–23, Gabriel gave Daniel the clarity to comprehend God's prophecy. In verse 24, he delineated the chronology of God's plan. In verse 25, he revealed the timeline for the first coming of Christ, followed in verse 26 by the reality of His crucifixion. Lastly, in verse 27, Gabriel revealed the cruelty and ultimate collapse of the Antichrist. Daniel had waited seventy years for the exile to come to an end and for Israel to be restored to its land. But Gabriel explained that though the people would soon return to their homeland, the ultimate deliverance of Israel would not be fulfilled at the end of those seventy years. Rather, God would complete His plan for Israel encompassing a period of 490 years, according to His fixed and irrevocable timeline.

THE COMPREHENSION OF DIVINE PROPHECY

Now while I was speaking and praying, and confessing my sin and the sin of my people Israel, and presenting my supplication before Yahweh my God in behalf of the holy mountain of my God, and while I was still speaking in prayer, then the man Gabriel, whom I had seen in the vision previously, touched

me in *my* extreme weariness about the time of the evening offering. Then he made *me* understand and spoke with me and said, "O Daniel, I have now come forth to give you insight with understanding. At the beginning of your supplications the word was issued, so I have come to tell *you,* for you are highly esteemed; so understand the message and gain understanding in what has appeared." (9:20–23)

Daniel began by recounting the features of the Lord's gracious answer. First, God answered Daniel **while I** [he] **was speaking and praying, and confessing my** [his] **sin and the sin of my** [his] **people Israel.** God displayed His grace by immediately answering Daniel's prayer **while** he was asking for forgiveness (**speaking and praying**) for the wickedness of his people. **Confessing** (cf. Dan 9:4) refers to the honest and open declaration of wrongdoing. As observed already, Daniel acknowledged his own (**my**) **sin** even as he acknowledged **the sin of** his **people Israel,** demonstrating his recognition that though he was faithful (cf. 6:10) he was no more worthy before God than his fellow Israelites (9:5). At the same time, he confessed that Israel, from its leaders to its laity (vv. 7–8) and from the past to the present (vv. 12–13), was guilty of high-handed crimes against God (vv. 10–11). He had to plead for mercy (9:15–20), and the Lord showed mercy, demonstrating the height of His grace, in contrast to the depth of Israel's depravity (cf. Rom 5:8).

God showed Daniel grace in that He answered when Daniel was still **presenting my** [his] **supplication.** The word **presenting** (lit. "to cause to fall") depicts that Daniel relinquished his requests to God. The Lord responded in lovingkindness, demonstrating Himself to be **Yahweh** the covenant-keeping **God** of Israel (cf. Exod 34:6–8). Daniel noted that God's revelation was in reply to his petition on **behalf of the holy mountain of my God,** referring to Jerusalem, the place where the temple had been built, and where the nations will ultimately come to worship the Lord in the millennial kingdom (Isa 2:2–3; Zech 8:3, 23). While God could have responded in wrath, He came to Daniel with the gracious revelation that He will fulfill Israel's destiny, blessing the nation and all the nations through Israel (cf. Gen 12:3). Because of God's grace in His unwavering commitment to Israel, Daniel called Him **my God.**

Second, God was gracious to provide Daniel further infallible revelation. In verse 21, Daniel repeated the phrase **"while I was still speaking in prayer"** to emphasize that God gave this revelation even before Daniel had finished confessing sin. While the previous verse exhibited God's grace despite Israel's sin, verse 21 explains what God's grace would accomplish. God sent **the man Gabriel, whom I**

[Daniel] **had seen in the vision previously.** Since Daniel **had seen** him in a prior **vision** (cf. Dan 8:15–16), he recognized this angel. In that vision, Gabriel appeared as a strong **man** who ensured that God's promises would come to pass. His name **Gabriel,** meaning "mighty man of God," accentuates that he was dedicated to carry out the purposes of God—including the prophecy of the seventy weeks.

Third, the Lord sent an angel to comfort and bring clarity to the weary prophet. The angel Gabriel **touched** Daniel just as he had done in the previous vision (cf. Dan 8:18). Daniel had collapsed in that vision, overwhelmed by God's power (cf. 8:18), and in the current situation he became faint **in *my*** [his] **extreme weariness.** Daniel was about eighty years of age and had humbled himself before the Lord in fasting, sackcloth, and ashes (9:3). Having deprived himself of all food and comfort to seek the Lord, Daniel had exhausted all his strength. **Weariness** denotes utter exhaustion, describing those who are famished (Judg 8:15; 2 Sam 16:2), lifeless (Isa 40:29), or incapacitated (50:4). Daniel's **weariness** exceeded common fatigue to the point of being **extreme.** In touching Daniel, Gabriel gave him supernatural strength to receive divine revelation as he had done previously. This was a restoration ministry similar to that of the angel from heaven who strengthened the Lord Jesus in His agony in the garden (Luke 22:43).

Daniel noted that Gabriel arrived **about the time of the evening offering.** God had commanded Israel to present an evening offering each day (taking place around 3:00 pm[1]) to dedicate themselves to Him (Num 28:1–8) and offer prayers to the Lord (Ezra 9:5; Ps 141:2). Additionally, God commanded Israel to offer sacrifices at that same time on the Day of Atonement (Exod 29:39–41) and Passover (Lev 23:5; Num 9:3). Significantly, the time of the evening offering was the time the Lord Jesus died on the cross (Matt 27:46).[2] Daniel prayed for God to forgive (Dan 9:19), and by answering at this time, God indicated that He heeded Daniel's prayer and would one day provide the perfect sacrifice for His people. The seventy-week prophecy, with its promises concerning atonement (9:24) by the death of the Messiah (9:26), was gracious new revelation in answer to Daniel's prayer.

Fourth, God graciously provided Daniel with the clarity he needed to comprehend this new revelation. Having strengthened Daniel, Gabriel **then made *me* understand and spoke with me and said, "O Daniel, I have now come forth to give you insight with understanding."** Throughout the book, Daniel sought to **understand** God's revelation (cf. Dan 2:17–19; 8:15, 27), seeking to comprehend the timing and circumstances of these prophecies (cf. 1 Pet 1:11). While God had unveiled many features (Dan 8:15–26), the timing was not yet revealed, leaving Daniel distraught to the point of saying, "There was none to make me understand it" (Dan 8:27). But Gabriel came to help the prophet **understand,** giving Daniel the answer to his distress. To assure Daniel that the answer would be sufficient, Gabriel also **spoke with me** [Daniel] **and said, "O Daniel, I have now come forth to give you insight with understanding."** In saying **"O Daniel,"** Gabriel addressed his hearer with compassion, assuring him that he would have not merely understanding but **insight** as well. **Insight** refers to precise knowledge and expertise, giving one the ability to discern specific facts and analyze details (cf. Deut 32:29; Pss 32:7; 64:9; Dan 1:4; 9:13). The seventy-week prophecy would grant Daniel clear **insight** into God's plan for Israel. As Gabriel explained, he had **now come forth,** graciously sent by God to deliver this revelation to the prophet.

Fifth, God's revelation of the seventy-week prophecy reflected His grace and love toward Daniel. Gabriel continued to explain that, **"At the beginning of your supplications the word was issued."** As Daniel pleaded with the Lord to listen to his prayer (cf. Dan 9:18–19), the angel relayed that God heard every word from the outset, and immediately answered by issuing a command to dispatch Gabriel. The phrase **"the word was issued"** literally means "the word went forth" and was also used to describe Gabriel who had "come forth" to Daniel (v. 22).

Gabriel continued by highlighting God's love for Daniel, saying, **"So I have come to tell *you*, for you are highly esteemed."** The pronoun **"I"** is emphatic as Gabriel stressed that God sent one of the highest-ranking angels **to** convey this message to the prophet. The Lord did this because Daniel was **highly esteemed,** a term used elsewhere to describe that which is deeply cherished (Gen 27:15), valued (2 Chr 20:25), and treasured (Dan 11:43). Because of Daniel's integrity before the Lord, he was prized both by men (Ezek 14:14) and by God.

God's gracious willingness to answer Daniel's prayer foreshadowed the gracious content of His message. The seventy-week prophecy was a gift of love to Daniel that brought clarity and comfort to this faithful servant of God. Having reminded Daniel of God's grace and love, Gabriel exhorted the prophet to **understand the message and gain understanding in what has appeared.** Daniel was instructed to **understand,** or seek to comprehend, the **message** of the seventy-week prophecy, which was intricate and required thoughtful discernment. In so doing, he would **gain understanding** about this revelation of the seventy weeks that **has appeared** and even receive answers to his vexing questions about past visions (cf. Dan 8:27). Gabriel's exhortation reinforced that while the seventy-week prophecy required Daniel's careful attention, it would yield stunning truth regarding God's grand plan for redemption.

THE CHRONOLOGY OF GOD'S PLAN

"Seventy weeks have been determined for your people and for your holy city, to finish the transgression, to make an end of sin, to make atonement for iniquity, to bring in everlasting righteousness, to seal up vision and prophecy, and to anoint *the* Holy of Holies." (9:24)

Gabriel revealed that God's plan for Israel involved **seventy weeks,** to be understood as seventy periods of seven. Since Daniel was thinking about years, even mentioning "seventy years" explicitly (Dan 9:2), Gabriel's reference to the **seventy weeks** in effect referred to years as well: seventy weeks of years. When Daniel wanted to speak of actual weeks, he used the literal phrase "weeks of days" (or "entire weeks"; cf. 10:2). Thus, the reference to **seventy weeks** (9:24) is intended to identify a period of time amounting to 490 years.

The significance of the numeral seven would have been familiar to Daniel's Jewish audience, since seven was inherent to various God-ordained festivals in Israel. Every seventh day was a Sabbath (Gen 2:3; Exod 20:8), every seventh year a Sabbath year (Lev 25:1–7), and every seventh Sabbath year heralded a year of Jubilee (25:8–22). The reason the Babylonian exile lasted seventy years was to grant the Promised

Land rest for all the missed years of Jubilee (see discussion on Dan 9:2; cf. 2 Chr 36:21). Thus, seventy years was heavy upon Daniel's mind. To Daniel, who desired the exile to come to a complete end at the conclusion of these seventy years, God revealed that His plan for Israel was longer than these seventy years—it was seventy times seven years.

Through Gabriel, God declared that this period of time had **been determined,** a term used only here in the Old Testament, conveying the idea of cutting or tearing. God not only chose the outcome for His people before the foundation of the world; He also foreordained it, cutting the entire path through history to ensure it would take place. The seventy-week prophecy revealed the fixed features of God's plan for Israel.

Gabriel proclaimed that these seventy weeks were ordained **for your** [Daniel's] **people and for your holy city.** Daniel had prayed that God would have compassion on His people regarding their desolation (Dan 9:18) and that He would forgive their sin (9:19). His petition included concern for God's **holy city,** Jerusalem, emphasizing the desolation of the city and its sanctuary (9:17–18) as well as his desire for its future glory among the nations (9:16–17). As he delivered this intercessory prayer, he grounded his petition on the fact that both his **people** and the **holy city** were called by God's name (9:19). God's honor was at stake in Israel's blessing.

The seventy-week prophecy provided both an expansive answer to Daniel's prayer and six monumental aspects of these seventy sets of seven years. The first three purposes are negative while the latter three are positive. Together, they sum up the fulfillment of God's plan for Israel.

First, God's work in the seventy weeks would **finish the transgression. Finish** conveys not only completion but also restraint (Gen 8:2; Exod 36:6; Num 11:28), causing an action to cease by holding it back (1 Sam 6:10; Isa 43:6; Jer 32:2). At the end of the seventy weeks, God promised to bring wickedness under divine control. **Transgression** refers generally to willful rebellion, but Daniel said **"the transgression"** to describe particularly the collective wickedness of Israel. The only other time the phrase **"the transgression"** is used in the Old Testament is in Daniel 8:13 to depict the flagrant crimes of the nation. While applicable to the world in general, the first purpose of the seventy weeks is specifically to remove sin from Israel. This will be fulfilled at Christ's return when the people of Israel will repent (Zech 12:10–13:1) and be spiritually transformed (Zeph 3:9). Globally, transgression will be restrained during the millennial kingdom as sin (Isa 11:9) and death (65:20) are curtailed and confined. The end of all transgression will ultimately be realized in the eternal state, since no trace of evil could even be present in the heavenly Jerusalem (Rev 21:25–27).

Second, the seventy weeks will **make an end of sin.** The verb carries the notion of sealing up, like sealing up a letter (1 Kgs 21:8). A document which is sealed is preserved, as well as finalized and fully executed (Neh 10:1; Esth 3:2; Jer 32:11). The promise to seal up sin reveals God's determination to terminate it in judgment. While the seventy weeks will result in God dealing with Israel's transgression, this period will also include God's judgment on all **sin** globally. In the end, the Lord will unleash His wrath on evildoers everywhere, bringing an end to sin as justice is served (cf. Isa 24:1–23; Zeph 1:7–18; Heb 9:26; Rev 19:11–21; 20:7–10).

Third, God will **make atonement for iniquity. Atonement** has the idea of covering or blotting out (cf. Gen 6:14) and refers to the complete satisfaction of God's wrath against guilt or **iniquity.** The word **atonement** is the same term used for one of Israel's major feasts, "the Day of Atonement" (Lev 16:10), which anticipated the ultimate sacrifice of the Messiah (cf. Lev 16; Isa 53:4, 11). The seventy-week prophecy emphasized this truth, declaring that the Messiah would be killed after sixty-nine weeks (Dan 9:26). Daniel had prayed for forgiveness, and the Lord assured him that Israel's redemption would be accomplished through the substitutionary death of the Messiah. Christ's propitiating work on the cross would be the only means by which Israel's sin would be removed (Isa 53:10–12; Zech 12:10–13:1).

Fourth, even as God promised to deal with sin, He also promised to **bring in everlasting righteousness.** Because this righteousness is **everlasting,** denoting both permanence and cosmic reach, it will pervade throughout the entire created order. When God judges in righteousness (Rev 19:11; cf. Matt 25:31–46; John 5:25–30; Acts 17:31; Rev 20:11–15), He will purify and transform this world (Pss 96:13; 98:2, 9; Isa 61:11), so that no corruption exists on His holy mountain (Isa 11:9) as His people dwell in perfect safety in a world that is as God intended (Mic 4:4; Zeph 3:13; Zech 8:3–5). Righteousness will dominate the millennial kingdom as Christ rules, but it will be the only reality in the eternal state. As Peter wrote, there will be a "new heavens and a new earth in which righteousness dwells" (2 Pet 3:13; cf. Rev 21:27).

Fifth, the seventy weeks will end with God's decree **to seal up vision and prophecy.** Just as a deed or a law was signed, sealed, and delivered (cf. Esth 3:12; Jer 32:11), so will God one day **seal up** all revelation because all that He promised will be finished, having been completely executed. At that time, there will be no more prophecy and no need for revelation because all of it will have been fulfilled. Gabriel described divine revelation as **vision and prophecy. Vision** refers to all that God supernaturally displayed to reveal His plan for the nations (Dan 2:28; 8:1), kings (4:5), and history (7:1), and it was seen not only by Daniel but also by other prophets, revealing God's agenda (cf. Isa 6:1–3; Ezek 1:1; Zech 1–6; Acts 9:10–12; Rev 4–5). In contrast, **prophecy** dealt with the predictions of the future (Dan 9:2) as well as their convicting exhortations (9:6, 10). The combination of **vision and prophecy** expressed the fullness of God's revelation, both foretelling and forthtelling, including history and theology. Gabriel assured Daniel that after the seventy weeks, everything God had revealed—including all that Daniel had beheld personally—would be accomplished. The fact that revelation would be sealed up and closed after this period demonstrates that every promise of God in every detail will be perfectly realized.

Sixth, the seventy weeks will climax with God's crowning achievement **to anoint *the* Holy of Holies.** This expression is elsewhere translated as "most holy" (cf. Exod 29:37; 30:10), referring not only to the Holy of Holies in the temple but also to that which is most sacred, pure, and dedicated to the Lord throughout the land. While this standard of holiness was commanded in the law (cf. Lev 2:10; 27:28; Num 18:9), its fulfillment will be realized exclusively in the millennial temple. Appearing also in Ezekiel 40–48, this phrase describes both the holiness of God's temple and its environs. Thus, in addition to the **Holy of Holies** of the millennial temple (Ezek 41:4), the mountain of Jerusalem (43:12) and the land surrounding the city (45:3; 48:12) will also be most holy. The **Holy of Holies** will be the epicenter of holiness in the millennial kingdom. Daniel was burdened to see that Jerusalem would be God's holy mountain (Dan 9:16), the center of worship in the world (Isa 2:1–4; 60:14; Zech 14:17). Comforting Daniel, God revealed that He would fulfill this promise.

The seventy weeks looked forward specifically to the time when the temple would be anointed, the ceremonial act of consecration for sacred service. This rite (**to anoint**) historically involved the pouring out of oil (cf. Exod 29:36; 40:9; Lev 6:13; Judg 9:8; 1 Sam 16:3; 2 Kgs 9:3) to designate a person or place as fit and set apart for a God-given task. By anointing the Holy of Holies, God will inaugurate and thereby commission it for operation in the messianic kingdom. This ceremony will be especially significant in that it will counteract the abomination of the Antichrist during the Tribulation (Matt 24:15) and the onslaught that will take place in and around Jerusalem when Christ returns (Zech 12:1–9).

The consecration of the most holy place will mark the time during which holiness and worship will fill the earth. In that era, even horses and cooking pots will be called "Holy to Yahweh" (Zech 14:20). The Hebrew root of **anoint** (*mashach*) is the same for "Messiah" (*mashiach*), which is fitting since the Messiah will be responsible for building and consecrating the temple (6:12). The construction and consecration of the temple will mark the fulfillment of the Davidic covenant (2 Sam 7:13) and God's workings for Israel in history (Zech 6:13–15). For this reason, the temple's inauguration will coincide with the Messiah's triumphant coronation, as Israel and the entire world gathers to Jerusalem to celebrate God's goodness and holiness. With this, Gabriel assured Daniel that God would answer his requests for the restoration of Israel.

THE COMING OF ISRAEL'S MESSIAH

"So you are to know and have insight *that* from the going out of a word to restore and rebuild Jerusalem until Messiah the Prince, *there will be* seven weeks and sixty-two weeks; it will be restored and rebuilt, with plaza and moat, even in times of distress." (9:25)

Gabriel continued by exhorting the prophet **to know and have insight,** in other words, to pay intense attention so that he would comprehend the seventy-week prophecy and all its ramifications. The seventy sets of seven years would commence **from the going out of a word to restore and rebuild Jerusalem.** Some have argued that this describes Cyrus' decree in 538 BC, but Cyrus' edict concerned the rebuilding of the temple and not the rebuilding of **Jerusalem** (cf. Ezra 1:1–2). Others have suggested that this prophecy denoted the return of Ezra in 458 BC (cf. 7:8–26). While this is possible, Ezra's return endeavored **to restore** the priesthood (7:1–5) and the holiness of the people (cf. 7:25–26; 9–10). The event that best coincides with the command both to **restore** Jerusalem and to **rebuild** its infrastructure is the return of Nehemiah in 445 BC (Neh 2:1–8). Nehemiah even used the same Hebrew root for "word," as did Gabriel, to describe the king's authorization to rebuild Jerusalem (2:18).

Gabriel explained that from the moment of that decree **until Messiah the Prince, *there will be* seven weeks and sixty-two weeks.** The coming of **Messiah the Prince** is the major feature of the seventy weeks God planned for His people. **Prince** emphasizes the royalty and authority of God's representative regent (cf. 1 Sam 9:16). Used for the Davidic king (or "ruler"; cf. 2 Sam 5:2; 6:21; 7:8; 1 Kgs 1:35; 2 Kgs 20:5), it is a fitting title to describe the ultimate Davidic king, the **Messiah.** Because the Messiah is described as the **Prince,** the seventy-week prophecy has in view His appearance as the coming King, which was fulfilled by the Lord Jesus when He rode into Jerusalem and was greeted with honor as Israel's King (Matt 21:1–11).

A total of sixty-nine sets of seven years—amounting to 483 years—would transpire from the time around Nehemiah's return to the moment of Christ's triumphal entry. God divided that period into two segments. The first was **seven weeks,** or forty-nine years. This period corresponded with the completion of Nehemiah's career in rebuilding and restoring Jerusalem, along with the conclusion of Malachi's ministry and the close of the Old Testament canon.[3] The second segment of **sixty-two weeks,** or 434 years, would then continue from that point on to the moment of the Messiah's triumphal entry.[4]

God's timing is precise. To see its astounding accuracy, two factors must be considered. The first consideration is that the Bible's prophetic calendar uses 360-day years rather than 365-day years.[5] In Genesis, each month is counted as thirty days totaling 360 days (Gen 7:11, 24; 8:3). In Revelation, the latter three and a half years of the Tribulation (forty-two months) are given as 1,260 days which also assumes a 360-day year (cf. Rev 11:2–3; 12:6; 13:5). Since the prophecy of Revelation expounds on the book of Daniel (7:25), Daniel also would have used a 360-day calendar. The second consideration is the Jewish calendar, which recorded the cycle of sabbatical years according to a 360-day period.[6] Taking into account these two factors, seven and sixty-two sets of seven years would run from 445 BC to around AD 30, the exact time of Christ's triumphal entry and crucifixion.

Daniel knew the importance of the Messiah, he prophesied about Him, and he hoped for His coming (Dan 7:9–13). God graciously revealed to Daniel the precise timing of the Messiah's arrival. Historians have observed that there was an increased messianic expectation at the time of Christ in part due to Daniel's prophecy.[7] This was even reflected in the New Testament (cf. Matt 2:1–2; Luke 2:25, 36–38; John 1:41; Acts 5:36–37; 21:37–38; cf. Matt 24:15, 30; 26:64; Mark 13:26; 14:62). The seventy-week prophecy, revealed to Daniel hundreds of years prior to Christ's first coming, was fulfilled exactly as God had foretold.

In the time between the decree to rebuild Jerusalem and the coming of the Messiah, God confirmed that the city would **be restored and rebuilt, with plaza and moat, even in times of distress.** Such reconstruction took place as the city's **plaza,** or town square, was laid down. Its **moat,** or a dry trench that surrounded the walls of the city, was likewise completed. With its defenses restored, the city would thrive not only in the good times but **even in times of distress.** In the first set of seven weeks, or forty-nine years, the Israelites faced grave opposition as they struggled to rebuild the city (Ezra 4–6; Neh 4; 6; 13:1–9). But troubling **times** would only grow worse. In the sixty-two weeks of years leading up to the Messiah, Israel endured various fierce trials from Medo-Persia, Greece, and Rome, as Daniel prophesied (Dan 7:2–8; 8:1–14; 10:10–21; 11; cf. Zech 9:11–17). Nevertheless, the city remained restored and rebuilt. The seventy-week prophecy set God's plan to a timeline, assuring Daniel that Israel would endure to the arrival of the Messiah.

THE CRUCIFIXION AND ISRAEL'S CALAMITY

"Then after the sixty-two weeks the Messiah will be cut off and have nothing, and the people of the prince who is to come will destroy the city and the sanctuary. And its end *will come* with a flood; even to the end there will be war; desolations are decreed." (9:26)

The seventy-week prophecy predicted not only the humble arrival of the Messiah but also His death. The Messiah would be killed **after the sixty-two weeks.** The preposition **after** places the Messiah's death following the seven and sixty-two weeks, but before the seventieth week mentioned in the next verse (cf. Dan 9:27). In other words, the Messiah's death would occur between the sixty-ninth and seventieth week, indicating that the seventieth week would not come immediately after the sixty-ninth week. There is a gap of time between these weeks. As later revelation establishes, the events of this gap pertain to "the times of the Gentiles" (Zech 9:1; Luke 21:24), a period the seventy weeks does not cover because those weeks are reserved for Israel whereas the gap period concerns the nations (Dan 9:24). Since the death of the Messiah takes place in the times of the Gentiles (Dan 2:31–43; Zech 11; John 18:31–32; 19:14–15; cf. Zech 14:1–2), it does not occur during the sixty-ninth week but **after** it, and long before the seventieth week.

While later revelation unveils that much will take place during this period, including the mystery of the church (cf. Rom 9–11; Eph 3:8–9), Gabriel focused on the fact that at a crucial moment of that period **the Messiah will be cut off,** referring to the Messiah's death (cf. Gen 9:11). In the Mosaic law, the term denotes a kind of execution and curse that severs one from covenant blessings and community (cf. Exod 30:38; 31:14; Lev 7:27; Num 19:20). Daniel predicted that the Messiah who would arrive as the Prince (cf. Dan 9:25) would then be executed as a criminal, enduring the punishment of God's indignation and wrath for the sins of His people (cf. Deut 21:23; Ps 22:1; Isa 53:9; Gal 3:13). Gabriel further revealed that the Messiah would **have nothing** in light of His ignominious death. His execution would degrade Him in disgrace (Isa 53:2–3). Such a violent and humiliating death fulfilled the prophecies concerning the suffering of the Messiah (Gen 3:15; Ps 22:1; 118:22; Isa 53), and provided a preview of Christ's death by crucifixion. Earlier, Daniel begged for God's forgiveness and for His wrath to turn away (Dan 9:16, 19), and God showed that His plan had made a way for that to be accomplished.

Following Christ's death, **the people of the prince who is to come will destroy the city and the sanctuary.** While the Messiah was earlier described as the "Prince" (cf. Dan 9:25), **the prince** mentioned in this verse (v. 26) is the Antichrist, the **one who is yet to come** and who will try to usurp the place of the true Prince. This **prince** is, in reality, the boastful horn of the fourth kingdom in Daniel 7 and the one typified by the horns of Alexander the Great and Antiochus Epiphanes in Daniel 8. Since he is the ruler of the fourth kingdom, his **people** refers to Rome (cf. 2:40; 7:7). They **will destroy the city and the sanctuary** of Jerusalem. Being used by God to judge Israel for rejecting Christ (cf. Zech 11:1–3; Matt 23:37–39; 27:25; Luke 23:28–29), Rome besieged the capital of Israel in AD 70 and ransacked both the city and its beloved temple, returning again in AD 135 to bring final devastation. The term **destroy** describes corruption and utter ruin, a fitting word since not one stone of the temple was left on another (cf. Matt 24:2).

Because Daniel lived through the destruction of Jerusalem in 586 BC, he would understand the ramifications of this prophecy. Since the **sanctuary,** the holy place, would be destroyed yet again, it would be some time before the Holy of Holies would be anointed (Dan 9:24). The Roman capture of the **city** of Jerusalem would inaugurate another exile for Israel, postponing their restoration, removing them from prominence, and continuing the era of the Gentiles (cf. 9:25). The mention of the **people of the prince who is to come** marked this people's destruction of Jerusalem in AD 70 as a momentous occasion that would set in motion events ultimately leading to the coming of the Antichrist (cf. Zech 11:16–17). God's judgment against Jerusalem had massive cascading effects, which are confirmed by later revelation (cf. Zech 11:6; Luke 21:20–24).

Emphasizing the effects of this devastation, Gabriel concluded that Jerusalem's **end *will come* with a flood.** Just as the waters of a flood completely engulf the land, so Rome would overrun Jerusalem and leave it barren (cf. Isa 8:7–8; 28:2; Nah 1:8). Such destruction would carry long-term ramifications, so that **even to the end there will be war.** The **end** refers to the end times, the period of the Tribulation (cf. Dan 11:35). Following Jerusalem's fall in AD 70, the world would face an era of continual conflict affecting Israel's state of suffering until the time of the Tribulation and the Antichrist (cf. Zech 11; Dan 9:24; Matt 23:37–39; Luke 13:34–35). Gabriel declared that for this period **desolations are decreed. Desolations** refer to that which is shockingly destructive, even to the point of making a location completely uninhabitable and a wasteland. It was used to describe Antiochus Epiphanes' sacrifice of a pig on the altar of the temple (Dan 11:31; cf. 1 Macc 1:37–59; 2 Macc 6:1–5).[8] It would be used of Jerusalem's destruction in AD 70 (Matt 23:38; Luke 21:20). It was also used to denote the ultimate desolation caused by the Antichrist who will blaspheme God (Dan 9:27;

12:1; 2 Thess 2:4). As Gabriel prophesied, there would be not just one but many desolations for the nation. These desolations **are decreed,** meaning "to carve out" or "to cut." God carved a clear path for these events from the time of Daniel through the sixty-nine weeks and the subsequent gap period leading up to the seventieth week.

THE COLLAPSE OF THE ANTICHRIST'S REGIME

"And he will make a firm covenant with the many for one week, but in the middle of the week he will make sacrifice and grain offering cease; and on the wing of abominations *will come* one who makes desolate, even until a complete destruction, one that is decreed, is poured out on the one who makes desolate." (9:27)

Bringing the prophecy to its climax, Gabriel focused his attention on that **one week,** the final week of the seventy-week prophecy. Just as each week of this prophecy was a set of seven years (see discussion on Dan 9:24), so this final week, known as the Tribulation (Rev 7:14), will be a period of seven years. Unlike the first sixty-nine weeks which were grouped together (seven weeks and sixty-two weeks, cf. Dan 9:25), the seventieth week lacks such a connection. This implies that the final week does not immediately follow the sixty-ninth week, supporting the conclusion that the chronology includes a period between the sixty-ninth and seventieth weeks. After the long period of wars and devastation following the sixty-ninth week (see Dan 9:26b), the Tribulation will commence. The exact moment is unknown, since no one knows the day or the hour (Matt 24:36; Mark 13:32; Acts 1:7). The Tribulation, also known as the Day of Yahweh, will come as a thief in the night (1 Thess 5:2).

The **he** in verse 27 refers to the prince who is to come, the Antichrist (cf. Dan 9:26). The destruction of Jerusalem in AD 70 set in motion the history leading up to the final Antichrist, so the Antichrist will appear in the final week as the head of the final iteration of a new confederacy of nations once part of the Roman Empire (cf. 2:40; 7:7). Establishing his power, the Antichrist **will make a firm covenant with the many.** Unlike Christ who will justify "the many" (Isa 52:15; 53:11–12), the Antichrist will overpower and subjugate **the many,** asserting his will by force (cf. Gen 7:18; Isa 42:13). This covenant will be made with Israel and it will prevail against all of Israel's foes so that there will be peace in the Middle East. Ezekiel prophesied that the Antichrist will provide stability and peace to such an extent that the nation will live in unwalled villages (Ezek 38:11). Just as Antiochus Epiphanes put Israel at ease for a time (cf. Dan 8:25), so the Antichrist will be

Israel's greatest champion for a brief season. Offering peace and safety **for one week,** that is seven years, the Antichrist will initially be welcomed as a hero to Israel. In return for his covenant of protective peace, Israel will pledge their allegiance to him, and he will aid them to rebuild the temple destroyed in AD 70 (cf. Rev 11:1–2; Dan 9:26).

But as Antiochus Epiphanes made deceptive peace treaties with Israel and the surrounding nations (Dan 11:21–35), so the Antichrist will forge only a false peace. Violating his covenant **in the middle of the week he** [the Antichrist] **will make sacrifice and grain offering cease.** The **middle of the week** is the half-point of the seven years, the three-and-a-half-year mark. Daniel later corroborated this calculation, stating that this period will be a time (one year), times (two years), and half a time (one half of a year; 12:7), a total of three and a half years. Revelation also affirmed this number, speaking of forty-two months and 1,260 days (Rev 11:3), or three and a half years.

The mid-point of the Tribulation marks a shift into what the prophets and the apostles call the Great Tribulation (Matt 24:21), the great and awesome Day of the LORD (Joel 2:31; Mal 4:5), and the time of Jacob's distress (Jer 30:7). This time will be initiated when the Antichrist **will make sacrifice and grain offering cease. Sacrifice** refers to the slaughtering of animals unto the Lord whereas a **grain offering** signifies the giving of grain or any gift to God (Lev 23:37–38). Combined, **sacrifice and grain offering** symbolize the totality of Old Testament worship. Though the Antichrist will help reconstruct the temple, thereby restoring Israel's offering system, he will ultimately cause sacrifices to **cease.** The word **cease** comes from the word Sabbath. Just as God ordained the Sabbath to conclude a week, so the Antichrist will attempt to end Israel's worship and destroy God's chosen nation.

Gabriel further declared that **on the wing of abominations** *will come* **one who makes desolate.** The combination of **abominations** and **desolate** alludes to the "abomination of desolation" spoken of later by Daniel (Dan 11:31; 12:11; cf. 8:13; Matt 24:15; Mark 13:14). The abomination of desolation refers to a heinous and deeply offensive act against God as illustrated when Antiochus sacrificed a pig on the altar of the temple (cf. 1 Macc 1:37–59; 2 Macc 6:1–5).[9] Antiochus' action prefigured the Antichrist's ultimate blasphemous wickedness when he comes **on the wing of abominations. Abominations** are things that are detestable, referring most often to idols (Deut 29:16; 1 Kgs 11:5, 7; 2 Kgs 23:13; Isa 66:3). Just as Antiochus blasphemed God by a vile sacrifice, so the Antichrist will blaspheme the Lord through idolatry. However, the Antichrist will not merely offend God through a single idol or a wicked sacrifice but through an abundance of **abominations.** He will establish an entire new religious system of perversions and assert himself as a god (cf. Dan 11:31; 2 Thess 2:4; Rev 13:5–6). The Antichrist will be swiftly ushered into absolute power **on the wing** of this new religious system, the culmination of all human depravity. The second half of the Tribulation will feature the greatest defiance against God in all of human history (Dan 7:8, 21; 2 Thess 2:4; Rev 13:1–10).

The Antichrist will attempt to usurp not only all religion but also all political power. Gabriel described the Antichrist as **one who makes desolate,** a word that denotes a destruction that makes cities uninhabitable (cf. Ezek 6:6) and the land barren (cf. Gen 47:19). The Antichrist will unleash a devastating campaign of violence against God's people, starving them (Rev 13:17), hunting them down (13:7), and killing them (20:4). As an earlier vision in Daniel prophesied, the Antichrist, the boastful horn of the fourth kingdom, will wage war against the saints and seemingly prevail (Dan 7:21). Uniting the entire world, the Antichrist will seek to make an end of Israel (Zech 12:3). In the last half of the Tribulation, the nation will face the threat of annihilation on a level they had never faced before (12:1–9; 14:2).

The Antichrist will continue his diabolical efforts **even until a complete destruction, one that is decreed, is poured out on the one who makes desolate.** Though the Antichrist's rampage will be fiercer than anything the Jewish people will have ever endured, its fullness will be restricted to the last half of the seventieth week. Just as God limited the vicious madness of Antiochus to 2,300 days (Dan 8:14), so will He also limit the Antichrist to 1,260 days. God never gives His people more than they can endure (cf. Matt 24:22; 1 Cor 10:13), even limiting daylight at that future time to protect His people (Matt 24:29). Because of His commitment to Israel, the Lord will bring the Antichrist to **a complete destruction,** an even more extreme word than "desolation," used to describe exhaustive and unrecoverable ruin (cf. Jer 4:27; Nah 1:8–9). While the Antichrist will bring immense desolation against God's people, the Lord will ultimately and utterly crush the Antichrist, throwing him alive into the lake of fire (Rev 19:20). Even during the worst time of human history, there will be hope. As Paul declared, "And then that lawless one [the Antichrist] will be revealed—whom the Lord Jesus WILL SLAY WITH THE BREATH OF HIS MOUTH and bring to an end by the appearance of His coming" (2 Thess 2:8).

Conveying the certainty of this ending, Gabriel proclaimed that such destruction of the Antichrist is **one that is decreed,** meaning "to cut out a path," as used in Daniel 9:26 to declare that desolations were "decreed." In the same way that God brought all prior desolations to an end, so will He surely terminate the Antichrist and his wicked regime.

Before the foundation of the world, God carved out an unchangeable path that history would follow to its end. The God who decreed desolations also decreed the end of the one who makes desolate.

That this total and sure destruction is **poured out on the one who makes desolate** affirms the ultimate victory of the Lord God. Previously, Daniel confessed Israel's sin before the Lord, acknowledging that God's curse had been "poured out" upon them like a deluge of water (Dan 9:11). At the end of the prophecy, the Lord assured Daniel that such divine indignation would be **poured out** on Israel's greatest foe. As God pours out His debilitating wrath upon the Antichrist at the end of the age, He will be upholding the promise He gave to Abraham to curse those who curse Israel (cf. Gen 12:3).

With the judgment of **the one who makes desolate,** the Antichrist, the epitome of all of Israel's enemies, God will liberate His people from all threat. So, while the seventy-week prophecy lays out many trials for Israel, culminating in the Tribulation and the Antichrist, it concludes by declaring that Israel's adversaries will come to complete ruin. At the end, Christ will return (cf. Rev 19:11–18), conquer the Antichrist (19:20), destroy Israel's enemies (cf. Zech 12:1–9; Rev 19:21), and cause all Israel to turn to Him in repentance (cf. Zech 12:10; Rom 11:26; Rev 1:7). Establishing universal and absolute peace,

Christ will usher in His millennial kingdom. At the completion of the seventy weeks, all of God's purposes for His people Israel and the city of Jerusalem will have been accomplished (cf. Dan 9:24). Christ will then be King over all the earth, and Zechariah's words will be fulfilled: "In that day Yahweh will be *the only* one, and His name one" (Zech 14:9).

ENDNOTES

[1] Gary A. Anderson, "Sacrifice and Sacrificial Offerings: Old Testament," *The Anchor Yale Bible Dictionary* (New York: Doubleday, 1992), 5:878; Jacob Milgrom, *Numbers*, The JPS Torah Commentary (Philadelphia: Jewish Publication Society, 1990), 239.

[2] Robert L. Thomas and Stanley N. Gundry, *A Harmony of the Gospels* (New York: Harper Collins, 1978), 246 n. 1 and n. 3; John MacArthur, *One Perfect Life: The Complete Story of the Lord Jesus* (Nashville: Thomas Nelson, 2012), 462 n. a; Darrell L. Bock and Benjamin I. Simpson, *Jesus According to Scripture: Restoring the Portrait from the Gospels* (Grand Rapids: Baker Academic, 2017), 496.

[3] John MacArthur and Richard Mayhue, eds., *Biblical Doctrine: A Systematic Summary of Bible Truth* (Wheaton, IL: Crossway, 2017), 119–26, 894;

Renald E. Showers, *The Most High God: A Commentary on the Book of Daniel* (Bellmawr, NJ: Friends of Israel, 1982), 123; J. Dwight Pentecost, "Daniel," in *The Bible Knowledge Commentary: An Exposition of the Scriptures*, ed. J. F. Walvoord and R. B. Zuck (Wheaton, IL: Victor Books, 1985), 1363.

[4] J. Paul Tanner, *Daniel*, Evangelical Exegetical Commentary (Bellingham, WA: Lexham, 2020), 581–87.

[5] Tanner, *Daniel*, 585.

[6] Ronald L. Eisenberg, *The JPS Guide to Jewish Traditions* (Philadelphia: Jewish Publication Society, 2004), 164–66.

[7] Marinus de Jonge, "Messiah," *The Anchor Yale Bible Dictionary* (New York: Doubleday, 1992), 4:777–88.

[8] Stephen R. Miller, *Daniel*, New American Commentary (Nashville: Broadman & Holman, 1994), 226.

[9] Miller, *Daniel*, 226.

BIBLIOGRAPHY

Anderson, Gary A. "Sacrifice and Sacrificial Offerings: Old Testament." In *The Anchor Yale Bible Dictionary.* Edited by David Noel Freedman, 5:870–86. New York: Doubleday, 1992.

Baldwin, Joyce G. *Daniel.* Tyndale Old Testament Commentary. Downers Grove, IL: InterVarsity, 1978.

Bock, Darrell L., and Benjamin I. Simpson. *Jesus According to Scripture: Restoring the Portrait from the Gospels.* Grand Rapids: Baker Academic, 2017.

Boda, Mark J., and J. Gordon McConville. *Dictionary of the Old Testament: Prophets.* Downers Grove, IL: InterVarsity, 2012.

Chisholm Jr., Robert B. *Handbook on the Prophets.* Grand Rapids: Baker Academic, 2002.

Chou, Abner. *I Saw the Lord: A Biblical Theology of Vision.* Eugene, OR: Wipf & Stock, 2013.

Davis, Dale Ralph. *The Message of Daniel.* The Bible Speaks Today. Downers Grove, IL: InterVarsity, 2013.

de Jonge, Marinus. "Messiah." In *The Anchor Yale Bible Dictionary.* Edited by David Noel Freedman, 4:777–88. New York: Doubleday, 1992.

Dempster, Stephen G. *Dominion and Dynasty: A Theology of the Hebrew Bible.* New Studies in Biblical Theology. Edited by D. A. Carson. Downers Grove, IL: InterVarsity, 2003.

Eisenberg, Ronald L. *The JPS Guide to Jewish Traditions.* Philadelphia: Jewish Publication Society, 2004.

Hamilton, James M. *With the Clouds of Heaven: The Book of Daniel in Biblical Theology.* New Studies in Biblical Theology. Edited by D. A. Carson. Downers Grove, IL: InterVarsity, 2014.

Goldingay, John. *Daniel.* Word Biblical Commentary. Revised edition. Waco, TX: Word Books, 1984.

Herodotus. *The Persian Wars.* 4 volumes. Translated by A. D. Godley. Loeb Classical Library 117. Cambridge, MA: Harvard University Press, 1920.

House, Paul R. *Old Testament Theology.* Downers Grove, IL: InterVarsity, 1998.

———. *Daniel: An Introduction and Commentary.* Tyndale Old Testament Commentaries. Downers Grove, IL: InterVarsity, 2018.

Hill, Andrew E. "Daniel." In *The Expositor's Bible Commentary: Daniel–Malachi*. Revised edition. Volume 8. Edited by Tremper Longman III and David E. Garland. Grand Rapids: Zondervan, 2008.

Kaiser Jr., Walter C., and Paul D. Wegner. *A History of Israel: From the Bronze Age through the Jewish Wars*. Revised edition. Nashville: B&H Academic, 2016.

Keil, C. F., and F. Delitzsch. *Commentary on the Old Testament*. Peabody, MA: Hendrickson, 1996.

Knauf, Ernst Axel. "Tema (Place)." In *The Anchor Yale Bible Dictionary*. Edited by David Noel Freedman, 6:346–47. New York: Doubleday, 1992.

Koldewey, Robert. *The Excavations at Babylon*. London: Macmillan, 1914.

Longman III, Tremper. *Daniel*. The NIV Application Commentary. Grand Rapids: Zondervan, 1999.

MacArthur, John. *One Perfect Life: The Complete Story of the Lord Jesus*. Nashville: Thomas Nelson, 2012.

MacArthur, John, and Richard Mayhue, eds. *Biblical Doctrine: A Systematic Summary of Bible Truth*. Wheaton, IL: Crossway, 2017.

Margueron, Jean-Claude. "Babylon (Place)." In T*he Anchor Yale Bible Dictionary*. Edited by David Noel Freedman, 1:563–65. New York: Doubleday, 1992.

Milgrom, Jacob. *Numbers*. The JPS Torah Commentary. Philadelphia: Jewish Publication Society, 1990.

Miller, Stephen R. *Daniel.* New American Commentary. Nashville: B&H Publishers, 1994.

Merrill, Eugene H. *Kingdom of Priests: A History of Old Testament Israel.* 2nd edition. Grand Rapids: Baker Academic, 2008.

Merrill, Eugene H., Mark Rooker, and Michael A. Grisanti. *The World and the Word: An Introduction to the Old Testament.* Nashville: B&H Academic, 2011.

Montgomery, J. A. *A Critical and Exegetical Commentary on the Book of Daniel.* International Critical Commentary. Edinburgh: T&T Clark, 1927.

Osborne, William R. "Babylon." In *The Lexham Bible Dictionary.* Edited by John D. Barry et al. Bellingham, WA: Lexham, 2016.

Pentecost, J. Dwight. "Daniel." In *The Bible Knowledge Commentary: An Exposition of the Scriptures.* Edited by J. F. Walvoord and R. B. Zuck. Wheaton, IL: Victor Books, 1985.

Plato. *Alcibiades.* Volume 8. Plato in Twelve Volumes. Translated by W. R. M. Lamb. Cambridge, MA: Harvard University Press, 1955.

Ritzema, Elliot. "Nebuchadnezzar." In *The Lexham Bible Dictionary.* Edited by John D. Barry et al. Bellingham, WA: Lexham, 2016.

Sack, Ronald H. "Nabonidus (Person)." In *The Anchor Yale Bible Dictionary*. Edited by David Noel Freedman, 4:973–76. New York: Doubleday, 1992.

Segal, Michael. "Rereading the Writing on the Wall (Daniel 5)." *Zeitschrift für die Alttestamentliche Wissenschaft* 125, no. 1 (2013): 161–76.

Showers, Renald E. *The Most High God: A Commentary on the Book of Daniel*. Bellmawr, NJ: Friends of Israel, 1982.

Sprinkle, Joe M. *Daniel*. Evangelical Biblical Theology Commentary. Bellingham, WA: Lexham, 2020.

Tanner, J. Paul. *Daniel*. Evangelical Exegetical Commentary. Edited by H. Wayne House and William D. Barrick. Bellingham, WA: Lexham, 2020.

Thomas, Robert L., and Stanley N. Gundry. *A Harmony of the Gospels*. New York: Harper Collins, 1978.

Waltke, Bruce K., and Charles Yu. *An Old Testament Theology: An Exegetical, Canonical, and Thematic Approach*. Grand Rapids: Zondervan, 2007.

Walvoord, John. *Daniel: The Key to Prophetic Revelation*. Chicago: Moody, 1971.

Widder, Wendy L. *Daniel*. Zondervan Exegetical Commentary on the Old Testament. Grand Rapids: Zondervan Academic, 2023.

Xenophon. *Cyropaedia*. 2 volumes. Translated by Walter Miller. Loeb Classical Library 52. Cambridge, MA: Harvard University Press, 2014.

INDEXES

INDEX OF SCRIPTURE

INDEX OF SUBJECTS

the
MACARTHUR
NEW TESTAMENT
COMMENTARY

THE MACARTHUR NEW TESTAMENT COMMENTARY series
is a verse-by-verse exposition of the New Testament that brings
the believer into fellowship with God. Written for pastor
and layperson alike, every commentary examines the history,
language, and theology of the text to provide an accurate
interpretation of each passage. The goal is for the believer to
understand and apply God's Word to daily life in order to be
conformed to the image of the Lord Jesus Christ.

JOHN MACARTHUR PUBLISHING GROUP
LOS ANGELES, CALIFORNIA